THE

LAND OF LIGHT

Professor Hilton Hotema

A Disciple of The Ancient Masters
of
Astrology, Anthropology, Biology, Psychology and Cosmogony

I SBN: 978-1-63923-472-1

Printed: August 2022

Cover Art By: Amit Paul

Published and Distributed By:
Lushena Books
607 Country Club Drive, Unit E
Bensenville, IL 60106
www.lushenabooksinc.com/books

ISBN: 978-1-63923-472-1

THE LAND OF LIGHT

- -

Testimonials of Readers of Hotema's Folios

"The Hotema Folios are great. I can't stop reading them. Please send #1 and #2 Folios by Hotema on Live Longer" -- W. H. of New York.

"Son of Perfection by Hotema is the best and most complete analysis I ever read of the secret of earth life and the method of individual redemption and 'Salvation.' This reveals not only the 'True Path' to 'Atonement,' but gives the lie to the frauds of all false teachings on this most important of all subjects -- The Human Soul and it's path to perfection." -- P. G., Calif.

"Rush another set of the Hotema folios. I'm lending the set I purchased to a friend, who says they are great." -- Wm. C. L., N.C.

"I have difficulty laying down the Hotema folios long enough to write you to say I received them. It is thrilling to read works of an intellectually advanced person and find line after line explaining the things as I have pieced them out in my own serious studies and meditations." -- A. E. B., Kansas

"Hotema's folios are really great. Please send Live Longer I and II by Hotema to my mother." -- C. P., Alaska

"Hotema's folios astound me with the information they reveal." -- T. P. McG., N.Y.

"I have just finished reading the Mysterious Sphinx. It is a jewel -- it is Light -- More Light and Further Light." -- E. D. B., Washington

"We consider Prof. Hotema one of the world's greatest teachers." -- Grant E. Hockens, N.Y.

"I have read Hotema's manuscript of his wonderful work on the Tarot. It seems that each new work Hotema writes is more revealing than the one before; and that is a gigantic accomplishment, for they are all masterpieces."

"This late work on the Tarot presents many new and startling ideas which I have never read before in any writings.

"We are slowly and gradually led into the realm of genius, and shown the answers to many profound anthropological and psychological problems that have perplexed the best scholars for ages.

"It was left for the mind of Prof. Hotema to correlate and analyze all existing data, as well as to decode the symbols and allegories of the Ancient Masters, and to reach and explain the facts and conclusions which are of immense value to mankind, both now and in the future.

"The interpretation of the ancient Tarot symbolism is a great work, possibly his greatest, and I was so thrilled by reading his manuscript that I shall order additional copies. I have already ordered four copies to be sent to me as soon as published." -- Wm. C. Lloyd, 310 N. Broad St., Burlington, N.C.

"I have read the Magic Wand (Caduceus) and learned more from it than my many years in one of the "Mystery" schools. How wonderful it would be if only more people would find the Light and Seek the Truth." -- Dr. A. M. J., Chicago.

"As a Spiritualistic Minister and Teacher, I have found that because of human ignorance and fear, only a few are strong enough to face the facts as Hotema has presented them. Having to unlearn what one has been taught that is false requires far greater effort than if one could start with a clean, blank sheet and place thereon the facts of Life." -- G. D. C., California

"Hotema is a thinker far above the best scientists, for he is not afraid to oppose them and show where they are wrong." -- A. F., California

"Hotema's Flame Divine surpasses everything I have ever read before and I'm studying it with unlimited enthusiasm." -- Mrs. H. R. F., Florida

"The Great Red Dragon is to me an answer to my unconscious prayer for Light in the darkness." — W. B. H., Iowa

"We think the Mystery of Man is the most wonderful writing we have ever read." — W. T., California

"A reader fan of mine sent me your book 'Mystery Man of the Bible'. For over 40 years my beliefs have been along the lines of your book, which I regard as the greatest literary masterpiece of all time. Anyone who has read or studied the bible is certainly missing the most important part of his education if he does not read this book, and I recommend it most highly to my friends and enemies alike. Every man, woman and child should read it.

"My substantial mailing list is available to you, free, as a public service I feel honored to have the opportunity to make, in order that the Word of this great book may be spread far and wide." — A. D. Barber, Managing Trustee, Barber Scientific Foundation, Washington, D.C.

PROLOGUE

That it might be fulfilled what was spoken of the Lord by the prophet saying, Out of Egypt have I called my son (Mat. 2:15).

To that statement Wm. McCarthy refers and says:

"The Christians, who go about with a fine toothed comb and a spy-glass searching for biblical prophecies, find (this) one in Numbers, chapter 27:17.

"There shall come a Star out of Jacob, and a scepter shall rise out of Israel, and shall smite the corners of Moab, and destroy all the children of Sheth.

"The coming of Christ, they (Christians) yell. Let's see: Christ had no scepter; he did not smite the corners of Moab, and, in fact, he did not come from Jacob, (for) God was his father" (Bible, Church and God, p. 284).

This event, so highly impressive to the Christians, draws attention to Egypt, whose people and past history were such a mystery to the Christian world until ──

· "The pick that struck the Rosetta Stone in the loamy soil of the Nile delta in 1796," wrote Kuhn, "also struck a mighty blow to historical Christianity. For it released the voice of a long-voiceless-past to refute, with a withering negative, nearly every one of Christianity's historical claims.

"The cryptic literature of old Egypt, sealed in silence when Christianity took its rise, but haunting it like a taunting specter after the third century, now stalks forth like a living ghost, out of the tomb, to point its finger of accusation at a faith that has too long thriven on falsity" (Who Is This King of Glory?).

Egypt, "the land of the Winged Globe," says the Masonic Encyclopedia, "the land of science and philosophy, peerless for stately tombs and magnificent temples, the land whose civilization was old and mature before other nations, since called to empires, even had a name" (Vol. 1, p. 232).

Christian readers will suffer a sickening shock as the follow us and learn the facts about the Egypt out of which "have I called my son."

We have been years in compiling this work, and consulted the best authorities on Egypt that we could find, and have excerpted freely from their writings, and especially from the valuable works of Dr. Alvin Boyd Kuhn, titled "Who Is This King of Glory," and "The Lost Light."

In his Prologue in the latter work, concerning which the President of the Illinois State Library Board said: "This book will be to religion what Darwin's work has been to science," Dr. Kuhn stated:

"The corruption and final loss of the basic meaning of these (ancient scriptures) has been, in the whole time, the greatest tragedy in human history.

"Like Shakespeare's tide, which, taken at the flood, leads on to fortune, but, omitted, casts all the rest of life in shoals and quicksands, the wreckage of the Esoteric Gnosis in the centuries following Plato's day, culminating in the debacle of all philosophical religion about the (end of) the third century of Christianity's development, and ushering in sixteen centuries of Dark Ages, has thrown all religion out of basic relation to true understanding and caused it to breed on endless train and persecution that more than anything else blacken the record of man's heroic struggle toward the light.

"The present (1940) most frightful of all historical barbarities owes its incidence directly to the decay (and corruption) of ancient philosophical knowledge and the loss of vision and virtue that would have attended its perpetuation."

Chapter I

UNITARIANISM

The Universe is a Unit. The Ancient Masters so regarded it, and their doctrine and philosophy was one of Unitarianism.

The God of the ancient world was the Sun. It was not until the 4th century that this was changed. Then the Sun God was transformed into the

SON OF GOD

The Christian Bible gives the world approximately fifty-four (54) hours of the life of this Son of God. His Father created the world in six days, and He saved it in less than five days.

These are the facts that have been unearthed by unprejudiced researchers after digging into the ancient rubbish for one hundred and fifty years.

The ancient doctrine of Unitarianism was based on Astral Light, which modern science calls Cosmic Radiation, and that doctrine was commonly called Astrology.

No work nor system of the ancient world that has come down to us, has been more bitterly condemned than Astrology, and yet time has proven that it is the only science the world has ever had.

This condemnation has been necessary in order to hide the source of Christianity. For Christianity is founded upon Astrology, and then to conceal that fact, the symbols have been personalized and the allegories have been literalized.

Astrology was a science in India for thousands of years before the Vedas were compiled.

The renowned magician and astrologer, Asuramaya, was born in Atlantis, thus testifying, upon the authority of the Puranas, to the very extreme antiquity of this Astral Science.

Ptolemy Philadelphus (309-246 B.C.), a learned scholar of his time, was surprised to find that Astrology was the central theme of all the religious systems of the ancient world.

In his desire to build up the stock of his great library at Alexandria, he offered rich rewards for all kinds of ancient scrolls. Wise men of all nations, impelled by their desire for the reward, journeyed to Alexandria with their choicest writings.

In this way Philadelphus succeeded in securing for his library some 280,000 of the most valuable scrolls of the ancient world.

By comparing the various scrolls of the different countries, he discovered that all of them had practically the same system of culture and education.

And why not? We have all come from the same source. The nature of Life and the constitution of Man are the same in all regions of the earth, and governed by the same law.

Inscriptions on stone tablets found in all parts of the world, indicate that the entire earth was colonized by people from one source, and that source, according to James Churchward, was the sunken continent of Mu or Lemuria.

The Bible itself mentions a time when the "whole earth was of one language and one speech" (Gen. 11:1).

In that day all systems and religion and philosophy were the same.

All systems of culture and education are copies of this one original system, which varies in different countries only as the customs and conditions of the people vary.

Traces of this one system have been preserved by inscriptions on stone monuments and temples of all races and all nations, in spite of the ruthless work of destruction conducted by the religious bigots, who seek to make their system appear as the only true one.

It was this destructive work that forced the Ancient Astrologers to preserve their wisdom by resorting to ways and means not understood by those who had not the Key.

By this secret system there has been preserved unto this day, the gist of the only true Science of Cosmogony, Anthropology, and Biology that the world has ever had.

EGYPT

For reliable data on the systems of the ancient world, we go to "the Land of the Winged Globe", the land of astrological science, "peerless for stately tombs and magnificent temples, whose civilization was old and mature before other nations, since called to empire, even had a name," says the Masonic Encyclopedia.

By the ancient Greeks, Egypt was called Aiguptos. This finally became Egypt.

The Bible calls Egypt the "Land of Ham" (Gen. 10:6; 14:5; Ps. 105:23, 27; 106:22).

In Ps. 78:51, appears mention of a "Tabernacle of Ham in Egypt."

Now, Ham appears as the son of Noah (Gen. 11:18), and he dwelt in the land currently called Egypt. This information appears in a tradition of the ancient Hebrews, who called the land Mizraim, who was the son of Ham (Gen. 10:6; 1 Ch. 1:8).

Ham had four sons: Mizraim, Canaan, Cush, and Phut. The land of Canaan lay adjacent to the land of Ham, and may have been the home of Canaan.

When Abraham was 75 years old, he left Haran for the land of Canaan (Gen. 12:4, 5).

Lamech, Noah's father, was 56 years old when Adam died. This gave Noah, thru his father, direct contact with the life and learning of Adam, which Noah passed on to his son Ham, who passed it on to his son Mizraim.

Thus, the line of contact extended back in an unbroken line from Egypt directly to Adam — from the land after the Flood to the land before the Flood.

A strange story appears to have been interpolated in the first nine verses of the 11th chapter of Genesis. It fails to harmonize with the rest of the chapter. The 4th verse mentions certain people as preparing to build "a tower, whose top may reach unto heaven."

At this time Noah was 602 years old, and some authorities assert that this "tower" was the Great Pyramid of Gizeh.

There was a definite reason why the men who compiled the Bible carefully omitted all direct reference to the Great Pyramid. That reason will appear as we proceed. It was planned that way for a certain purpose.

The evidence uncovered by archeologists shows that many ages before the biblical Moses saw the light of day, the Land of Ham was noted for stately tombs and palatial temples, and the center of the greatest Science of Creatology, Anthropology, and Biology that the world has ever known since the sinking of the continents of Atlantis and Lemuria.

After the sinking of those two continents, Egypt became the axis round which rolled the Ancient Arcana as it passed from the East to the West and met in the land of Ham.

Words Cut In Stone

But the arrival of the despots was expected, and was described in the famour prophecy of Hermes, who said:

"O Egypt, there shall remain of thee for future generations only fables that no one will believe; nothing of thee shall endure save the Words Cut In Stone."

And it was so.

· The history of the Land of Ham extends back into distant antiquity, and vanishes completely in a cloud of obscurity. The Christian army of bigots and fanatics did their destructive work well and thoroughly.

Until 1895, the oldest records found in Egypt reached back only to the 4th Dynasty.

Since then, there has been a steady stream of surprising discoveries in prehistoric and early historic cemeteries; and due to these discoveries, monuments already known, and such as the annals of the Palermo Stone, have been made to speak for the beginnings of Egyptian history.

Due to immense excavations and investigations in recent years, the people of ancient Egypt have become better known to us by their work than any civilization which preceded Greece.

That primitive history of Egypt has been preserved because it is carved on stone that has resisted the ravages of time and the hand of the bigots.

In spite of the fact that its stone monuments have been cleared of the accumulation of the ages, and its hieroglyphs deciphered, the occult knowledge of the Egyptian Masters is still known to only a few, and they, for the sake of safety, keep silent. They have no desire to be burned as witches.

House of Enoch

The Masters who designed and built the Great Pyramid of Gizeh were not produced in Egypt.

The ancient Hebrews had a tradition that the Great Pyramid was built 300 years before the biblical deluge, and that the names of Seth, Enoch, Noah and Shem appeared on the roster of the builders.

The Egyptian "Book of the Dead" stated that the leader was Enoch. The Egyptian transliteration of the word Phoenix is Pa-Hancock, or "House of Enoch."

Prof. Thevenin adduces evidence to show that thousands of years ago, there suddenly appeared in Egypt from some unknown land, scientists and philosophers with a knowledge of astrology, astronomy, geometry, chemistry, physics, mathematics and mechanics so extraordinary, who had scientific instruments of such precision, who understood Cosmogony so well, and who employed their knowledge so skilfully, that their work is still miraculous and beyond our comprehension.

Joseph, noted Jewish historian, born in 37 A.D., gives it as an historical fact that Seth, Adam's third son (Gen. 5:3), and his immediate descendants, "were the inventors of a peculiar sort of wisdom concerned with the celestial bodies and their order.

"That their knowledge and inventions might not be lost before they were sufficiently known, upon Adam's prediction that the world was to be destroyed, they built two pillars, one of brick, the other of stone, and inscribed their discoveries upon them both, so that in case either pillar was destroyed by the Flood, the other might remain and exhibit these discoveries to mankind.

"Now, this (pillar) remains in the land of Siriad (Egypt) to this day."
— Jewish Ant., 1, 2.

That pillar of stone is said to be the Great Pyramid of Gizeh.

The ancient Arabians had a similar tradition. In a scroll preserved in the Bodleian Library, Abou Balkhi said:

"The wise men, before the Flood, foreseeing the coming of a catastrophe, either by submersion or by fire, which would destroy all created things, built in Egypt many pyramids of stone, to have some refuge against the approaching calamity.

"Two of those exceeded all the rest in height, being 400 cubits high, and as many broad, and as many long. They were built of large blocks of marble, and so well joined together that the joints were scarcely perceptible. Upon the exterior of the structures were inscribed every charm and wonder of physics."

Massoudi, another Arabian author, relates the same information, even more circumstantially, and said that:--

"On the eastern or Great Pyramid, built by these ancient men, the celestial spheres were inscribed, likewise the positions of the stars and their circles, together with the history and chronicles of past times, of that which is to come, and of every future event."

Another Arabic fragment, claiming to be a translation from an ancient Coptic scroll, gives a similar account of the origin of the Pyramids, and stated that:--

"Innumerable precious things were treasured in these structures, including the mysteries of science, astrology, astronomy, geometry, physics, and such useful knowledge" (p. 173).

Still another Arabian account states that the Pyramids were constructed by Hermes, the same person as Enoch, father of Methuselah (Gen. 5:19-25), to preserve the arts and sciences and other knowledge during the Flood.

One legend states that Hermes, also known as Enoch, was the Master Architect who planned and supervised the building of the Great Pyramid. He made it a complete dramatization of the fundamental essentials of sidero-geological, physical, psychological, astral and historical wisdom. He embodied in it the sciences of mathematics, geometry, astrology and astronomy, which were regarded as the foundation of all science, philosophy and religion.

Pre-Flood Knowledge

The knowledge and wisdom accumulated by Noah and his predecessors before the Flood, when men were said to have lived almost a thousand years, Noah would not leave behind to be destroyed by the Flood.

So, to preserve this ancient wisdom, this wise man of the antediluvian world, or some of his immediate descendants shortly after him, if not in his lifetime, built the Great Pyramid.

Of necessity, therefore, the science which fashioned this giant edifice possessed knowledge and tools which came from the grand world before the Flood, and found imperishable memorial in this Monument of the New World. Hence, if not built by Noah, by Seth, and the Sethite antediluvian patriarchs, there was still a direct link between it and them, between their science and that which it represents.

It is certain that the profound prophetic, astrological and philosophical wisdom embodied in and represented by the Great Pyramid, required thousands of years for its discovery and development. It could not possibly have been discovered and developed by the Egyptian natives. Nor has any one ever claimed that it was.

Modern man has only recently reached that stage in cosmic science which enables him just to begin to decipher and understand some of the simpler parts of the strange message of the Great Pyramid.

That is the reason why this ancient structure, with which men have for centuries believed themselves acquainted, has suddenly burst forth with a light so dazzling and a science so gripping as to convert the scoffers into sober believers, and to convince scholars and scientists that it can be accounted for only on the theory that a Master Scientist of great antiquity was the Architect and Builder.

The Great Monument

Chronologically, the Great Pyramid antedates by thousands of years all present nations and faith, including the most ancient writings in the Christian Bible. In fact, those writings are comparatively recent.

It is not only the massive masonry of the Great Pyramid that merits so much attention, but the space around which this giant structure was built to endure the passages of time and the ravages of the elements.

It appears that within the restricted area of this Monument is contained the most startling story ever written of the Earth's history, of the mysteries of the Universe, of Creation, and of man's place in nature.

A written record may be easily forged, altered, or interpolated. But a stone structure could not be changed without the changes being instantly detected. For any alteration would mean a mutilation of the masonry, as has occurred in the face of the Sphinx.

The church fathers tried to batter up and destroy the Sphinx, but the Stone Symbol of the Four Elements was too much for them.

Every prophetic element embodied in the Great Pyramid is far older than any part of the written Bible. As the two works in general often tell similar stories, it is certain that the biblical scribes had intimate knowledge of the Great Pyramid.

Then why did they so deliberately and completely fail to make any direct and definite reference to it?

To that question would come an amazing answer if it could issue from the lips of Constantine's "correctores" who compiled and "revised" the books of the Bible.

Direct reference to the Great Pyramid was cautiously deleted from the Bible, which was compiled and edited so as to deceive the masses and future generations.

It was in the plot to have the time come when the masses would despise Egypt. For the scheme was to sink Egypt so low that it would be stigmatized the "Land of Darkness."

We steal what a man has, then murder him to conceal the crime.

LAW OF CYCLES

As the Ancient Masters discovered that man's body is the Temple of the Solar Spark, it was logical that they made an important branch of their science the teaching of how to keep that Temple in the best of order. For the reception and transmission of Solar Force requires a healthy body.

Solar Force cannot function normally thru abnormal bodies. An electric globe must be in perfect order to receive and express the electric force flowing into it, or else the force produces no apparent effect.

The Book of the Master says: "And thus, throughout the teachings of the Egyptian Mysteries, the Visible Light was but a shadow of the Astral Light; and in the wisdom of that ancient country, the Measures of Truth were the years of the Most High."

"The adorable Fire and immense depth of Flame which the human heart must not fear to touch, is that power proceeding from the Giver of Life, the Glorious Sun" we are told.

The astronomical change in the dispensation of the Astrologers is termed the Precession of the Equinoxes.

This is a retrograde motion in the passage of the Sun as it crosses the ecliptic each year.

The Equinox was observed by the Astrologers to move at the rate of 1 degree in 72 years.

This movement makes the place of the Sun, at the beginning of the astronomical year, appear to retrograde thru the Zodiakos 1 degree in 72 years, completing the circle about 72 x 360 degrees equal 25,920 years, or 25,868 to be exact.

This cycle of 360 degrees is divided by 12 into sections corresponding to the zodiakol signs, each section containing 30 degrees. When we divide 25,868 by 12 we have 2,156 years as the duration of one subcycle, or Age as it is called.

Thus it will be observed that it required a vast period of time for the Astrologers to check and recheck this data thru the ages, in order to formulate their chart and prepare their records, showing and describing not only these mysteries of the Universe, but also the conditions of the Earth and its inhabitants, as affected by the vibrations of the various Celestial Bodies symbolized in the Zodiakos,—all of which the dictionaries, histories and encyclopedias, prepared under the censorship of the Mother Church, declare is false, counterfeit and spurious.

Facts Concealed and Distorted

Histories, encyclopedias and works of modern science state that the Zodiakos "seems to have originated with the Chaldean astronomers about 2100 B.C."

That statement is utterly false, and those who make such statements are either falsifying or disregarding the facts. It is a case of falsifying to hide the facts.

As further evidence of the flagrant manner in which modern science works "to save face" by concealing ancient knowledge, it is said in a book of 818 pages, published in 1941, and titled "Marvels and Mysteries of Science," that it was Hipparchus who discovered the "precession of the Equinoxes in 125 B.C." We quote:

"The Greek astronomer, Hipparchus, who has been called the father of astronomy, discovered in 125 B.C. the precession of the equinoxes by comparing the length of the year, determined by dates when certain bright stars could first be seen in the dawn after the sun had passed them in its annual motion, with the length of the year of the seasons determined with the gnomon.

"This amazing discovery of a motion of the earth that requires nearly 26,000 years for the completion of one circuit, sometimes called the Great Year, could not be explained at one time, but had to wait 1800 years for the mind of Newton to explain the physical cause." (p. viii).

More lies and falsehoods fed to the Christian world.

That "amazing discovery" was destroyed by the Mother Church to make the Christian world believe its claims that the Ancient Astrologers were "superstitious heathens."

The equinox passes thru the 30 degrees corresponding to each zodiacal sign, and this gives rise to the Age of that sign.

The equinox, or place of the Sun at the beginning of the astronomical year, retrograded by "Precession" back from the first constellated Aries, which is the beginning of the Circle of Stars, 30 degrees, and therefore into the space corresponding to the sign Aquarius, in 1881.

That is the time of the beginning of the Aquarian Age in which we now are. And as the mental and astral forces received by humanity are different when the Sun's place among the stars at the beginning of the year corresponds to the place of the different zodiakol signs, it gives some idea of the type of civilization that, past or future, exists while the equinox is in any sign by multiplying 2,156 years by the number of signs removed from Aquarius, and adding to or subtracting from, the year 1881.

We now reach an interesting theory which may have no valuable practical application, but shows how far advanced the Astrologers were in the mysteries of the Universe.

That is, the obliquity of the ecliptic is constantly changing, a fact known to the Astrologers and only discovered by the moderns.

This refers to the fact that the Pole of the Earth is moving in an orbit at right angles to the earth's diurnal rotation at the rate of about 1 second every 2 years, or 1 degree in 7200 years.

Should the earth continue this motion, it would turn completely polarwise in 7200 x 360 or 2,592,000 years. And as turning around completely equatorwise is called one common day, so turning completely around polarwise is called one polar day.

According to modern astronomers, the earth does not thus turn completely over polarwise; but after moving 3 or 4 degrees, it starts to swing back, according to known laws, which causes it thus to wobble.

As the time involved to observe this swinging back was so great, some Astrologers concluded this polarwise motion continued uniformly on around the circle, so they based the larger periods of duration on this false Polar Day of 2,592,000 years.

It is asserted that the days of creation mentioned in the Bible actually refer to these Polar Days of immense duration.

The Polar Day was known to the Egyptian Masters, and its duration was incorporated in the Great Pyramid of Gizeh. But just because the amount of average movement of the earth Polarwise was included in this monument, does not warrant us in concluding that they believed the earth completely to turn over, as this movement over a few degrees, even though it swings back, is actually one of the most important astronomical movements, having a profound effect upon the climate and other matters on the earth.

And it is this average movement of 1 degree in 7200 years which the Great Pyramid records.

It was the Ancient Astrologers' knowledge of the precession of the equinoxes that constrained them to divide the Zodiakol Circle into 30 degrees. And they knew the exact annual amount of precession down to the fraction of a minute.

Nor did they have "to wait 1800 years for the mind of Newton to explain the physical cause."

However, if Newton did explain it, his explanation does not appear in the book titled "Marvels and Mysteries of Science," -- a title that should be changed to the Marvels and Mysteries of the Universe.

There are no marvels and mysteries about "science". So-called scientists are strong on throwing bouquets at themselves.

In 4,588 B.C., the Sun entered the zodiakol sign of Taurus, the Bull; and for 2,156.67 years the Bull was the object of veneration. The Bull, in turn was succeedec by Aries, the Ram, when the Sun entered that sign in 2,432 B.C.

And here we discover the origin of the Lamb of God (Jn. 1:29).

From 2,432 B.C. until 276 B.C. the Ram, or "Lamb of God," became the object of adoration when, in its turn, it opened the equinox for 2,156.67 years, "to deliver the world from the wintry reign of cold, barrenness and darkness," as the ancient nations termed it in their annual celebrations.

During those centuries, the people living north of the Equator called Aries "The Lamb of the Sun God which taketh away the evils of the world" (Jn. 1:29).

The annual "birth of the Sun" was widely celebrated, for 2,156.67 years, by all ancient nations north of the Equator on that day, which day has now come to be the 25th of December, the birthday of the gospel Jesus, and so well commercialized that it constrains the foolish people of the U.S.A. to squander millions of dollars each year.

Known By Their Fruits

If primitive man were an ape or a troglodyte, or the Stone Age creature pictured by science, or the superstitious heathen as claimed by the Mother Church, how could the builders of the Great Pyramid in prehistoric days have known enough even to make and handle the tools, machines and expedients indispensable in the construction of an edifice so enormous in dimensions, so massive in its materials, so exalted in its heights, and so perfect in its workmanship, that unto this day it stands without a known rival on earth?

How could such primitive, ignorant, unlettered men have known the spherity, rotation, diameter, density, latitudes, poles, land distributions and temperatures of the earth, or its astronomical relations?

How could such primitive man have solved the problem of squaring the circle, or determining the four cardinal points?

How could they know of the grand precessional cycle, the length of its duration, the number of days in the true year, the mean distance of the sun from the earth, and the exact position of the stars when the Great Pyramid was built?

How could they devise a standard system of weights and measures, so evenly fitted to each other, so beneficently conformed to the common wants of man, and so perfectly harmonized with all the facts of Nature?

How could they know how to put all these things on record in one single structure of stone, without one verbal or pictorial inscription, yet proof

- 14 -

the
CONSTELLATION of

against all the ravages and changes of time, and capable of being read and understood down to the very end of the world?

Yet all these things these Ancient Astrologers did, and did know, and proved it by their work.

There stands that amazing knowledge recorded in solid stone and displayed to the eyes of the world, challenging the scrutiny of all the experts and scientists on the earth.

Scholars, scientists, religionists, evolutionists,--they may sneer, but they cannot laugh down this mighty piece of masonry, nor scoff its angles, proportions, measures, nature references, and cosmic correspondence which its builders gave it.

There they stand in all their speaking significance, stubborn and invincible beyond all the power of modern man to suppress them.

Nothing can blot out that amazing record. And it is written in stone and true astral dignity of the Ancient Astrologers, fashioned in the image and likeness of the Universe, and illumined and impelled of the Living Fire to make this memorial of man's sacred possessions, ere they should finally be lost amidst the continuous deterioration, degeneration, debauchery, and corruption of humanity.

It is a record whose antiquity none can dispute, whose authenticity none can corrupt, and whose secrets none can construe without the Key of the Ancient Astrologers.

And that Key is contained in the Ancient Tarot.

UNSOLVED MYSTERIES

This is the modern age of steel and cement, believed by many to be the end of progression in that direction.

And here appears a baffling problem connected with the cement used by the Masters in building the Great Pyramid.

That cement could be reduced to the consistency of paint, and yet made to hold for centuries with such tenacity, that the rocks break rather than the joint.

Chemists can analyze it, but no scientist can produce it. Modern science is not so modern.

Another mystery as great relates to the drills and saws used to cut the granite blocks.

Among the reasons why the Coffer or lidless Chest in the Great Pyramid is a veritable miracle in stone, and the profoundest single object in the world, are the spiral markings of the drill used to hollow out its interior.

To drill out granite thus, as a carpenter bores out wood, requires not only a drill of extreme hardness and toughness, but a machine permitting overhead pressure ranging from one to two tons.

That the scientists who built the Gread Pyramid had and used such drills is a fact established by the evidence of the character of the work done. For in no other way could be made the spiral markings as they appear in that solid granite Coffer.

And every Mason knows what that Coffer is, what it means, and for what it was used.

And here is more evidence to indicate that the ancient engineers used some form of atomic energy in their work.

Evidence also appears that the mechanics operated bronze saws having hardened teeth, set with sapphires. In other instances, the cutting edges must have been set with diamonds.

But this is just a mere fragment of the whole truth--only the faintest ray of light on a mystery that the world would be glad to unravel if it could. Its explanation would undoubtedly disclose more valuable secrets.

The press of August 20, 1936, described a subway system, used by the Astrologers ten thousand
between the second pyramid and the Sphinx, "carved thru hard sand stone, (and) about eight feet in height," said the account, which added:

"The causeway is more than 70 feet wide (and):the central division was a covered road, down which the priests marched on ceremonial occasions."

In the center of the subway is a deep shaft that ends in a large room, in the center of which is another shaft that descends to and ends in a roomy court, flanked with seven side chambers, some of which contain huge sarcophagi of basalt and granite.

In one of the seven rooms is a third shaft extending to a side chamber.

Total depths of the three shafts is more than 125 feet.

Modern engineers assert that these giant structures, cut in solid stone, are strong evidence to show that the ancient engineers used some form of atomic energy, and were so cautious about their secret that they were careful to leave behind no trace of their devices and mechanisms.

To support this assertion they cite the case of John W. Keely who astonished a group of men in 1888 when he gave a demonstration of his machine powered by atomic energy.

In 18 minutes he cut a tunnel in hard gold-bearing quartz that was 18 feet long and 4½ feet in diameter. He refused to divulge his secret, and later destroyed his machine and his secret died with him.

It is well to add some information here unknown to the modern world. After Christianity was established in the 4th century, the Roman army, headed by Catholic Priests, gathered up two ship-loads of these ancients machines and devices, carried them out into the Mediterranean sea and sank them.

That is the reason why there was not found any trace of these mechanisms.

Book Of The Dead

For almost 3500 years no human voice disturbed the ghostly silence of the interior of the Great Pyramid, after the despots had assassinated the Masters who were unable to escape.

In all those centuries no eye beheld by the light of a torch its hidden passages and chambers. For in all those centuries no one was able to discover the entrance, so perfectly had the builders fitted the hinged, limestone door that swung inward at the bottom, and with no great effort.

It is doubtful whether it had ever been discovered without the aid of the data contained in the Egyptian "Book of the Dead."

The Great Pyramid's chronology is based upon the precessional cycle of 25,920 years. This cycle of time began 7,100 years before the days of the biblical Adam.

The Pyramid's system of astronomical science is so profound, comprehensive and purposeful, as to transcend anything that the mind of modern man may devise.

Some scholars think the Pyramid was built in some past Aquarian Age by Astrologers who possessed the science that enabled them to solve the mysteries of Creation, and who sought to preserve that knowledge by concealing it in symbols that constitute measured revelations, or revelations thru measurements.

The earth entered the Cycle of Aquarius in 1881. It takes the earth 2160 years in its great circuit to pass thru the range of a Constellation of the Zodiakos, of which there are twelve.

The previous Aquarian age ended 25,950 years ago. If the Great Pyramid was not built then, the next preceeding Aquarian Age extends back almost 26,000 more years, or about 52,000 years from now.

And that is the age some scholars have fixed as the time when the Great Pyramid was built.

Pyramidal Facts

The Great Pyramid is the most accurately orientated structure on earth today. It varies only five seconds from the true north and south position; and even this slight variation, engineers believe, has resulted from a shifting of the earth's surface since the structure was built.

The pyramid engineers divided the Circle into 360 degrees, and we have copied their system because we were not able to improve on it. They used the "pyramidal inch" because it was the equivalent to a primitive Diameter Inch. This was the unit of measurement adopted by the Hebrews.

As we approach the interior of the structure with a tape measure of Polar Inches or British Inches, it begins to speak in its sign language of "revelations through measurements," disclosing the story of past ages before it was built, of the days when it was built, and of the ages yet to come.

It is said that modern engineers are unable to construct geometrically a square equal in area to a given circle. But the Antechamber of the Great Pyramid shows that its builders squared the circle.

A circle whose circumference equals the number of days in the year can be "rolled" from the center of the Antechamber to the end-wall of the King's Chamber, exactly 365.242 pyramid inches.

The squaring of the circle is related, then, to the "rolling of a circle on a line or flat plane."

A circle rolled one-eighth of its circumference to the right and left of a center line, defines the exact shape of the Apex or chief corner and headstone, and the full form of the Great Pyramid (Ps. 118:22; Mat. 21:42; Mk. 12: 10; Lu. 20:17; Acts 4:11).

Certain lines of measurement in the Great Pyramid reveal the true solar year of 365.242 days, and the sidereal year by the measurements of 36,525.6 inches.

Science has found that certain measurements of the Great Pyramid represent the solar cycle and also the difference between the solar, sidereal, and orbital years, thereby resulting in measurements that give the average distance of the sun from the earth, the earth's surface displacements, and the displacements of the earth's orbit.

The ancient men who did that are the ancient men whom the church has found much pleasure in referring to as "superstitious heathens", then destroyed their scrolls in order to hide the facts and truth from the world.

The "measured revelations" of the Great Pyramid show that its engineers not only knew the distance of the earth from the sun, but the length of the solar year to the exact fraction, the length of the sidereal year, and the position of the pole star, the weight and rotundity of the earth, the length of the earth's axis, the parallels of latitude, that the earth revolves around the sun, and numerous other scientifically known and demonstrable facts which scientists have discovered only within the last two centuries.

The Greeks, presented in the encyclopedias by the church as being so wise, estimated in 500 B.C. that the distance of the sun from the earth was approximately ten miles. They later raised it to 2000 miles. Finally, they fixed the distance at 2,500,000 miles.

At the close of the 16th century, Kepler increased the figure to 36,000,000 miles.

It was not until 1908 that modern science, after a decade of study, fixed the "average distance of the earth from the sun at approximately 92,900,000 miles".

Knowing the results of modern man's long struggle with this vast problem, it is amazing to learn that thousands of years ago, the Great Architect who supervised the building of the Great Pyramid, built into its base the plans which give the distance of the earth from the sun as 92,996,085 miles.

Dr. P. Lowell said: "The Great Pyramid was a grand observatory, the most superb one ever erected.

"The Grand Gallery's floor exactly includes every possible position of the Sun's shadow at noon from the year's beginning to its end.

"We thus reach the remarkable result that the gallery was a gigantic gnomon or sundial, telling not only like an ordinary sundial, the hour of the day, but on a more impressive scale, the seasons of the year" (Precision of the Pyramids, p. 90).

The facts appear to show that the Great Pyramid, built more than fifty thousand years ago- some forty-five thousand years before God had created the earth according to the Bible, represents not only a civilization that had no infancy known to us, and whose work and art are so vastly superior to all that followed, but likewise a language so perfect in terminology as to permit technical calculations, exact specifications and explanatory instructions positively indispensable to a task as tremendous, difficult and artistic as the Great Pyramid.

The evidence unearthed shows that the Great Pyramid anticipated by thousands of years all the natural laws of "gravitational" astronomy that have been discovered and advanced by Kepler, Newton, Laplace, Einstein, and all the other modern scientists.

It required the discoveries of modern science to teach us these things, and to reveal some of the wonderful wisdom that was lost to the world, when the church burned the ancient libraries and scrolls in order to plunge the people of the Roman Empire into darkness.

Simply as an architectural achievement, this Pillar of Stone (Isa. 19:19, 20), has held its high place at the head of the list of "The Seven Wonders of the World." And under the studies of the engineers, astronomers, mathematicians, Egyptologists and Divines, it has recently come to assume a character vastly more remarkable.

Facts and coincidences so numerous and extraordinary have been evolved which the most sober philosophic minds have been startled by them.

For it would verily seem that it were about to prove to be a Key to the Universe itself--a symbol of the profoundest facts of science, truths of philosophy, and of all the past and future history of humanity. At least, many competent scholars have been constrained so to regard it, after the most thorough sifting that the appliances of science have been able to give it.

This information comes as quite a humiliating blow to the egotistical scientists who have believed that we, in this civilization, st   at the very peak of human development and knowledge.

As we continue to advance, we are able to discern the footsteps of those Ancient Masters who trod the Path of Light long ages before us; and we are learning that they were then familiar with all the mysteries of the Universe which science has discovered in the last five hundred years.

We praise the discoveries of Copernicus, Galileo, Kepler, Newton and Laplace, and many other highly endowed men of the last few centuries, and we praise them none too highly when we pay glowing tribute to their grand work.

But as we progress and learn more, we can see that the Geocentric and Heliocentric Systems of Astrology and Astronomy were known to the Ancient

Masters hundreds of thousands of years ago.

And still modern works on these subjects allege that "the older system of astrology had as its foundation the supposition that the Earth was the center of the Cosmos, and that the mighty bodies of the fixed stars, no less than those of the system now known as the Solar System, moved around the Earth as though it were their stationary and governing center" (Heliocentric Astrology, by Yarmo Vedra, p. 10).

That statement is untrue and absurd.

After it had burned the ancient libraries and ancient scrolls, then the Mother Church instituted the postulate that the Earth is the very center of the universe, and the sun and all other celestial bodies revolved around it.

When Copernicus revealed that the Earth revolves round the Sun, hilarious parties were held by the church to discredit him, in which the reveling Christian fanatics would pretend they were too dizzy to walk upright -- for who could keep his balance on a revolving Earth?

Chapter II

ATOMOLOGY

When modern science succeeded in cracking the atom, it was surprised to find that Atoms, long considered as the ultimate of Matter, are actually constituted of whirling Sparks of Astral Light, Living Fire.

Then science promptly boasted that, in this achievement, it had gone deeper into Matter and advanced farther in the realm of the unknown than man had ever gone before.

Archeologists have discovered that more than fifty thousand years ago the Masters had a perfect system of symbols, similar to the biblical symbols, for what modern science terms "nuclear fission."

For almost two millennia, scholars have tried to interpret these symbols, and failed because their knowledge was insufficient for the task.

Before science uncovered the secret of the Atomic Bomb, we come first to the greatly ridiculed postulate of the ancient alchemists regarding the Transmutation of Metals -- a theory long scoffed by scientists.

With the discovery of "nuclear fission,' gold money suddenly went out of circulation by act of the National Congress, and it even became illegal, under the new law, for one to possess gold money.

Only these atomic scientists knew the reason why. They had discovered, with profound surprise, that the ancient alchemists' allegation as to the Transmutation of Metals was not so silly as modern science had believed.

When these shocked atomic scientists discovered that the Transmutation of Metal is a fact, they hastily notified the President of the United States, Franklin D. Roosevelt, -- and that is the reason why gold went out of lawful circulation.

Gold will remain out of circulation only so long as this knowledge endures. That will be of brief duration. A few centuries maybe. Then the secret will again be lost.

It is said that the Egyptian Tarot contained in symbolism the secret of nuclear fission, and even stated the kind of metal required, -- radium, symbolized by the planet Uranus.

The feat is performed by tremendous electric voltage. The Ancient Masters knew how to do it, and they did it.

And furthermore, these Masters knew what occurs within the atom to cause it to break up or disintegrate. They understood the underlying principle.

Like all great achievements, the most puzzling problems become simple when the basic principle is understood. Even the ailments of man.

That is the reason why a certain doctor, in 1944, was silenced. He died suddenly in jail of "heart attack." He paid with his life for getting too far ahead of medical art.

That is the common practice, and extends back into the dim past. Ye know nothing at all, nor consider that it is expedient for us (doctors), that one man should perish in order to save medical art (Jn. 11:50, 51).

Then the deceived, mind-controlled masses ask why the Masters don't come out in public and teach the mysteries of Life.

History constantly repeats itself because human nature never changes.

As we study the symbolism of the Ancient Masters, finally destroyed in the 4th, 5th and 6th centuries by the Mother Church, we are amazed to see the wealth of knowledge they possessed.

In taking a certain degree in the Ancient Mysteries, the lips of the neophyte were lightly touched with a live coal of fire, the interpretation of which is: In due time the masses of the earth will be scorched by a terrific conflagration of their own making.

It seems the answer to that one has appeared -- the Atomic Bomb.

Every Mason should know, but they do not, that the Living Fire is symbolized by "the strong grip of the Lion's Paw" that "raised" (energized) Grand Master Hiram Abiff (History of Freemasonry, p. 181).

The Living Fire is symbolized by Leo in the Zodiakos.

Also, that the symbolical "den of lions" into which it is claimed the "early Christians" were thrown, is pure allegory.

As they understood life, evolution, cosmic law and human nature, the Masters knew approximately what the condition of the earth would be now.

While the earth is constantly changing, as Hotema shows in Cosmic Creation, certain factors and principles remain the same.

The Masters knew that human nature never changes. What man has always done, he will always do. He would work his own destruction in the future just as he has done in the past. And the Masters even knew by what means this would occur. So they wisely deferred the fatal event as long as they could by concealing the secret from the masses and despots.

Now, read history again, and learn how ancient civilizations have disappeared, and left behind no trace to explain the reason why.

Modern man, in his deceptive "progress," is approaching the final stage. Already his latest discoveries have filled him with terror. He has come too close to the Infinite Power of the Universe. Not the church God, but the Mighty Atom.

As man envisages the dangers of his new discovery, he is horrified by what he has found. He has been taught by the church to look to a God in the sky and tremble at the thought of the approach of the Last Judgment, and now he finds that the Omnipotent Atom is the Master of the Universe.

With this knowledge before us, we learn the reason why the Masters so carefully concealed cosmic secrets from the unscrupulous despots, and the unreliable and irresponsible multitude.

To understand the Science of Man, we must know the secrets of the Universe. And to know these secrets puts into man's hands a power to great for any but the tried and tested Initiates.

The Masters understood the Science of Man because they knew the secrets of the Astral World. In their scrolls they described the Science of Man in symbols[7] and parables, fable and fiction, in order to preserve it for the race, and to conceal it from those unworthy to have it.

Land of Darkness

The great Land of Light and Learning becomes the Land of Darkness.

One writer says, "Why Egypt was called the 'Land of Darkness' is difficult to understand. There are many lands on earth that at one time rose to great heights, and then sank to a very low level; but none of these is commonly referred to as the 'Land of Darkness.' " -- Symbolic Prophecy of the Great Pyramid.

There is a story back of this that the Mother Church has tried hard to keep concealed from her dupes and slaves.

When the facts are known, the answer is easy to find. Livingstone had the answer in his work, "Book of David," under the subhead "The Constantine Bible" (p. 140).

He knew who founded the Roman Catholic Church, why it was established, and who directed the task of compiling the book called "Word of God."

When Constantine "the Great" had gained the throne of the mighty Caesars, like most other despots, he craved more power.

He was motivated by the vain ambition to have the exclusive religious power of the world. He would go to the seat of the religion which ruled most of the subjects of his vast realm, import that religion to Rome, revise and alter it to serve his purpose, invent a popular name for his new religion, and then conceal his fradulent work by sending out his army to demolish the ancient temples and to collect and destroy all the ancient scrolls that could be found.

To make his work the more secure, effective, and complete, he would murder the Masters of the ancient religion, and then discredit them and disgrace their country by stigmatizing it, "Land of Darkness."

When this Roman despot and his successors had finished their nefarious designs, the grand Land of Light and Learning was actually transformed into a "Land of Darkness." Its temples were demolished, its scrolls were destroyed, and two shiploads of its precious instruments and equipment were dumped into the sea.

It was the most astounding crime ever committed against humanity in all the known history of the world; and its consequences and reactions were so broad and vast, that it plunged the Roman Empire into a state of intellectual darkness that is still in evidence in Europe and America.

For this "good work", Constantine, the murdered, was the first person to be elevated to the plane of "Saint" by the blighting institution which that "good work" created.

Out of that darkness and desolation has come all the history of ancient days that the Christian world has had until the last two centuries.

When it became less dangerous to do so, archeologists began to salvage from the ruins of the "Land of Darkness" some precious fragments of the Lost Wisdom of the Ancient Masters.

Facts Suppressed

The actual facts of this crime have been suppressed as much as possible by the Mother Church.

The Science of Cosmogony, Anthropology and Biology of the World before the Flood, brought to Egypt by Enoch, Seth, Noah and Shem, and preserved from loss and destruction in the Great Pyramid, remained unknown to the modern world until the 19th century, thanks to the Mother Church.

Our scientists, philosophers and theologians, reared and schooled in the intellectual darkness created by the "good work" of Constantine and his successors, have known so little about the basic sciences of the Universe, that they were unable to decipher the ancient symbols and inscriptions on the monuments and temples of stone in Egypt.

Had not the Wisdom of the World before the Flood been thus preserved, it had been forever lost. We would have practically no alternative but to believe as true the baseless claims of the religionists, scientists, and evolutionists, that modern man stands at the peak of human development and progress.

A century ago scholars said that "the more the subjects of ancient Egyptian mythology and symbology were studied, the less they knew about them."

-23-

The reason of this is clear. That mythology and symbology related to Cosmogony, Anthropology and Biology, whereas we had been led to believe by the church that it dealt with actual gods and saviors.

Recent discoveries of the researchers into Egypt's ruins began in 1858, and have unearthed a mass of startling knowledge, concealed for sixteen hundred years in the strange hieroglyphs on the ancient tablets and stone monuments, which no one could interpret because the Key was lost.

The Rosetta Stone

When Archbishop Chrysostom, in the middle of the 5th century A. D., made the boastful statement that --

"Every trace of the old philosophy and literature of the ancient world has vanished from the face of the earth,"

and that the Papacy, as --

"The ghost of the Roman Empire, sat crowned on the grave thereof,"

it appeared that man was lost in a world of darkness out of which he would never be able to work his way to the Light, if the church could prevent it.

A character in a modern drama made the observation that, "Money is made in the dark."

Christianity was born in the dark and lives and thrives on darkness.

One author said, "We can easily forgive a child who is afraid of the dark. The real tragedy of life is when religion is afraid of the Light."

The symbology and allegory of the Bible, meaning little to the laity and lying far beyond the ability of the preacher to interpret, seemed like they would never give up their secrets to the world.

All this was suddenly changed in 1799 by the shovel of a trench-digger that unexpectedly struck the Rosetta Stone in the soil of the Nile delta.

For that shovel struck a fatal blow against the Mother Church at the very close of the 18th century.

When Col. Broussard dug up the Rosetta Stone, Napoleon wisely saw its possible value.

It may be that, for direct cultural value to all races dominated by Christianity, no event, battle nor reformation in human history surpasses that single discovery of an entablatured rock.

That rock is rapidly proving the ghost of retribution, the instrument of justice, the Nemesis of a religious system promoted by darkness, fostered by ignorance, and supported by superstition.

The message of that rock opens up the vast treasure-house of ancient Egyptian literature, which presents the full and incontestable evidence of Christianity's false claims.

That literature supplies the missing link in the body of comparative religious study which proves beyond all cavil that Christianity is not the first pure, divine release of the one "true religion," but only a badly mangled copy and mutilated form of ancient Egyptian drama.

In the year 195 B. C. the Egyptian Masters erected this stone in honor of Ptolemy V. Epiphanes. It is 3½ feet long, 2½ feet wide, nearly a foot thick, and carved into its surface was an inscription, duplicated in three languages, in the Greek, in the Egyptian Hieroglyphics, and in the common Egyptian tongue.

But for the discovery of that stone, the history of ancient Egypt might still be buried in the ruins of its towns and temples, demolished by the Roman Army under the leadership of Roman Catholic Priests, as they reduced the Land of Light and Learning to the "Land of Darkness."

By comparing the Greek translation of the stone with the Egyptian, the French scholar M. Champollion, in 1822, was able to discover the Key to the fundamental principles of the ancient Egyptian Hieroglyphics, and to begin, for the first time in modern history, a decipherment of the mysterious, long-dead, unknown language of Seth, Enoch, Noah and Shem.

And so, the lost history of Ancient Egypt began to unfold before the staring eyes of the startled world.

Champollion's labors released the Ancient Voice which Chrysostom had believed was silenced forever, and which Voice refuted with a withering negative practically every one of Christianity's historical claims.

The startling story told by the stone amazed the world and shocked the Mother Church.

The church authorities always rush in and take possession of all ancient scrolls that may be discovered, in order to keep their true messages from the masses. But the Rosetta Stone escaped them.

The cryptic literature of ancient Egypt, sealed in silence by the Church Fathers when Christianity was being built, began to haunt the Church like a taunting specter, and stalked forth lik- a living ghost out of a dark tomb, to point its bony finger of accusation at a system that has far too long lived in darkness and waxed fat on ignorance.

For that literature, out of oblivion, now rises up to proclaim the true source of every dogma and doctrine of Christianity as being Egyptian, the product and heritage of a remote antiquity.

After the discovery of the Rosetta Stone came the translation of the Egyptian --

1. Book of the Dead
2. The Pyramid Texts
3. The Book of Thoth (Tarot)

which laid open to the world the irrefutable data which showed that, far from being the First Gleam of Light in a world said to have previously been benighted in heathenish darkness, Christianity was only a poor, crippled orphan, appearing without the evidence of its true parentage and sadly belying in its external form, the semblance of its ancestral lineage.

The precious scrolls of ancient Egypt now unroll the sagas of wisdom which announce the inexorable truth, that not one single doctrine, rite, tenet or usage in Christianity was a new contribution to world religion; but that every article and particle of that system was and is a disfigured copy of ancient Egyptian mythology, symbology and allegory.

Christianity, it proclaims, not only failed to register one single advance in any line of wisdom, but deplorably vitiated and disfigured the beautiful structure of Cosmogony, Astrology, Anthropology and Biology which it ignorantly adopted and wretchedly purveyed as its own alleged new creation.

The ghostly shadow that pursued Christianity with the semblance of external similarity for sixteen hundred years, now resolves into the substance of verifiable proof of original identity.

The entire body of Christianism is now seen to be nothing more than crudely revamped and horribly mutilated Egyptianism.

The ancient parentage which it strove so desperately to hide and deny, and the marks of which it so sedulously endeavored to obliterate in the early days of its existence, now rise up from the dead past out of that "Land of Darkness" to charge its ungenerous offspring with faithlessness and deceit.

The Christian Bible, the creation legend, descent into and exodus from Egypt of the "Children of Israel," the ark and flood allegory, the "history of the Israelites," Hebrew prophecy and poetry, the gospels and epistles, are all now proven to have been the transmission of Egypt's scrolls into the hands of later generations, which knew neither their origin nor their fathomless meanings.

Long after Egypt's voice, expressed thru the inscribed hieroglyphics, was hushed in silence, the perpetual relics of Hamitic wisdom from the World before the Flood, with their cryptic message utterly lost, were dragged forth and presented to the world by parties of ignorant zealots as a new body of facts and truths.

Egypt's "Christ" was not an actual man. It had been equally fatal to Christianity had he been.

The fact of his symbolism now rises out of the past which the Church Fathers thought they had sealed in oblivion forever, to strike the death-knell of a false and spurious religion.

The "gospel life" of the Christian Jesus is nothing more than the garbled, distorted, fragmentary copy of an Egyptian prototype who existed only as a symbol, a purely dramatic figure, portraying the nature of Life and the Constitution of Man.

With this single revelation of lost truth, the structure of historical Christianity crumbled into ruins.

So long as the voice of ancient Egypt's wisdom was hushed in silence, so long as the Egyptian symbols could not be made to speak, the pious imposture of the Church Fathers could continue unchallenged.

The Rosetta Stone and Champollion's remarkable work in deciphering its cryptic hieroglyphics, reveal in ancient Egypt's wisdom the ancient origin and long-denied parentage of Christianity.

Christianity can no longer support its claims in the face of contradictory evidence which, with the release of Egypt's hidden wisdom, the recovery of the lost language of symbolism in which all ancient scrolls are written, and the recovery of the buried esoteric meaning of all ancient religion, has increased in volume from hillock to mountain size.

Chapter III

LAND OF MYSTERY

Why has the Christian world called Africa the Dark Continent and Egypt the Land of Darkness?

There is "method in this madness." It has been done to turn the world against and away from that region which contains the ancient secrets of Cosmogony, Anthropology and Biology which the church has tried to hide from a deceived world.

The Ancient Masters of Egypt had said, "As above, so below." As the Macrocosm, so the Microcosm.

While the strange system of Seth, Enoch, Noah and Shem remained a mystery until the last century, after a hundred years of study which revealed almost nothing, that system has begun to give up startling information, and to describe things so peculiar to us, that there is much we do not yet know about it.

When we search thru histories and encyclopedias for data on these things, we find little but falsehoods and deception that have been prepared for us by the church.

These histories and encyclopedias, rigidly censored by the church, assert that the knowledge and invention that made Egypt famous, were taken there by the Greeks.

The facts being discovered reveal just the reverse to be true.

It was in this "Land of Darkness" that Thales (640 B.C.), Pythagoras (582 B.C.), and other great Greek philosophers acquired their education. The record shows that Pythagoras studies under the Egyptian Masters for 22 years; and still they did not teach him all they knew.

Few nations ever received more from other countries than Greece received from Egypt; and none appear to have been more tenacious of the pretense that all their attainments originated with themselves.

The Greeks said the Egyptian Masters had three systems of expressing their thoughts.

"The first was clear and simple, the second was symbolic and figurative; and the third was scientific and hieroglyphic. The same terms assumed, at their will, either the literal, the symbolical, or the transcendental. Such was the genius of their language" (Pike).

Heraclitus indicated this difference when he designated the language of the Egyptian Masters as speaking, signifying, and concealing.

In the theogonic and cosmogonic sciences, the Egyptian Masters used the third method in writing. Their hieroglyphics had three corresponding and distinct meanings. The two latter could not be understood without the Key.

These Masters alone possessed the Key to the cosmogonic, anthropologic and biologic sciences which are symbolically and allegorically mentioned in the Bible, but understood by no one without the Key.

The Christian clergy have never been able to make sense out of the symbology and allegory of the last book of the Bible, because they deal not with gods and crucified saviors as taught by the church, but with certain psycho-bio-physiological processes of man's body that are still beyond the ken of modern science.

The student will find an interpretation of that symbology and allegory in "Son of Perfection," by Hotema.

Christian theologians are profoundly ignorant of the true meaning of the symbols and allegories in the Bible.

Some authors assert that the first settlers of the Nile Valley concealed their past history from the world. That is erroneous. It was destroyed by the church to conceal the source of its theology.

The finer arts never attain perfection quickly. At all times and in all lands they have passed thru a long line of crude attempts and imperfect beginnings before they reached perfection.

This is not so in the case of Egypt. In Egyptian art and science there is no trace of such a beginning. They burst upon us at once in the full bloom of their highest perfection, indicating clearly that they must have been brought there from other regions by other races.

As the despots who rule the world control its history, the masses have little opportunity to learn what the despots do, and what they have done, to keep their subjects and slaves in darkness and ignorance.

The history books and encyclopedias are more or less unreliable, as the material prepared for them must pass censors before being published.

The modern study of the science and philosophy of ancient Egypt really began with the publication in full of the texts, both hieratic and hieroglyphic, of the Heliopolitan, Theban, and Saite Recessions of the Egyptian "Book of the Dead," and of the cognate funeral texts, such as the "Book of the Underworld," the "Book of Breathings," and "Book of Transformations," the "Lamentations," and the "Festival Songs of Isis."

And even here, the workers and writers, prejudiced by the theory of Evolution, and pressurized and intimidated by the Christian clergy, have suppressed, deleted, distorted, and perverted many facts which, if truly and fully known, would demolish and destroy the current dogmas, doctrines, opinions, beliefs and faith, and disclose the terrible "skeleton in the closet," which the Mother Church has striven for more than sixteen hundred years to hide from the eyes of the world.

Were it possible or practicable to teach publicly the ancient science of Cosmogony, Anthropology, Biology and Psychology, it would produce a New Age and a New Race. The Mother Church would sink and medical art would perish and vanish.

The ruins of the Masters' architecture in the "Land of Darkness" has been the school of modern builders. From the wonders of that land which the ravages of time and the elements have spared, we may conjecture with reasonable certainty as to what has been destroyed.

In Constantine's "Land of Darkness", there still proudly standing because its very gigantism made it invincible to all the wrath and fury of Christian fanaticism to destroy, is one of the most amazing works that man has ever produced, so far as the world knows.

It seems certain that the greatest wisdom of the world stood there, and was present in the designation and construction of the "signs and wonders in the land of Egypt," and the placing of them there by "the Great, the Mighty God," says the Bible (Jer. 32:18-20).

And so, the church God gets great credit as an imaginary entity that does nothing.

The Great Pyramid is so huge and so unconquerable, that not even the Roman Army, led by the Roman priesthood, could budge it from its base.

And that Temple of Stone in Constantine's "Land of Darkness," before which eminent engineers of the modern world stand in awe and wonderment, was erected so far back in the dim past, that all record and memory of its birth have been lost and destroyed.

Of the vast antiquity of Constantine's "Land of Darkness," that brilliant Englishman, Winwood Reade, wrote:

"Buried cities beneath our feet; the ground on which we walk is the pavement of a tomb. See the pyramids towering to the sky (Gen. 11:4), with men, like insects, crawling round their base; and the Sphinx, couched in vast repose, with a ruined temple beneath its giant paws.

"Since those huge mountains of stone were raised, the very heavens have changed. When the Ancient Masters began their work, there was another Polar Star in the northern sky, and the Southern Cross shone upon the Baltic shores.

'How glorious are the memories of these Ancient Wise Men, whose names are long since forgotten; for they lived and labored in the dim, distant, unwritten past. Too great to be known, they sit on the heights of the centuries and look down on their fame. Their Work is so perfect that it seems to have been directed by some Master of the Universe."

That is a brief sketch of the Glory of the Masters whom the Mother Church has taught the modern world for sixteen hundred years to believe that they were nothing more than superstitious, heathenish idolators.

He who knows the facts and continues to support Christianity, is a traitor to his own conscience and to the human race.

Chapter IV

HERMETIC MAGIC

In ancient Egypt it was that Magic attained to the grade of completion as a cosmic science and was formulated as a perfect doctrine.

As a summary of all the dogmas that obtained in the ancient world, nothing equals those few paragraphs graven on precious stone by Hermes, and denominated the Emerald Table, in substance as follows:

Unity of being and unity in harmony of all things, according to the ascending and descending scales; progressive and proportional evolution of the Word J H V H (Four Elements); immutable law of equilibrium and graduate progress of universal analogies; correspondence between the idea and its e pression providing a measure of likeness between the Macrocosm and the Mi cosm; essential mathematics of the infinite, proven by the dimension of a single angle in the finite: all this is expressed by the one proposition, "that which is above is like that which is below, and that which is below is like that which is above, for the fulfilment of the wonders of the one thing."

Hereunto was added by Hermes, the revealing and illuminating description of the Creative Agent, the Pantamorphic Fire, the cosmic medium of occult force, -- in a word, the Astral Light which modern science has recently discovered and calls Cosmic Radiation.

That was the God of the ancient world, and so stated in the Bible in these words: "For our God is a Consuming Fire" (Heb. 12:29).

In this connection Eliphas Levi wrote: "Let us go further and affirm the existence of a Fire which abounds in images and reflections.

"Term it, if you will, a superabundant Light which radiates, which speaks, which goes back into itself.

"It is the flaming courser of Light, or rather it is the cosmic agent that overcomes and breaks in that astral steed.

"Picture all as vested in flame and emblazoned with gold, or think of him naked as love and bearing the arrows of Eros.

"But if thy meditation prolongeth itself, thou wilt combine all these emblems under the one form of the Lion.

"Thereafter, when things are no longer visible, when the Vault of Heaven and the expanse of the universe have dissolved, when the stars have ceased to shine and the lmap of the moon is veiled, when the earth trembles and the lightning plays around it, invoke not the visible phantom of Nature's soul, for thou must in nowise behold it until thy body has been purified by the Holy Fire.

"When thou dost behold the Sacred Fire with dancing radiance flashing formless through the depths of the whole world, then harken to the Voice of Fire" (History of Magic, p. 67).

After calling Fire Astral Light, Levi continues:

"Clairvoyant ecstasis is a voluntary contact of the Ego with the Universal Fire, or rather with that Light, abounding in images, which radiates, which speaks, and which circulates about all objects and every sphere of the universe. ...

"Having attained the power of direct reading in the Light, the adept became a seer. Then, having established communication between the Light and his own will, he learned to direct the former, even as the head of an arrow is set in a certain direction.

"He communicated at his pleasure to the Ego of others; he established intercourse at a distance with those fellow-adepts who were his peers; and, in fine, he availed himself of that force which is represented by the Celestial Lion.

"Herein lies the esoteric meaning of those great Assyrian figures which hold vanquished lions in their arms. They have discovered the secret of Astral Light.

"The Astral Light is otherwise represented by gigantic sphinxes having the bodies of lions and the heads of Magi.

"Considered as an instrument made subject of intellectual power, the Astral Light is that Golden Sword which Mithra used in his immolation of the sacred bull. And it is the arrow of Phoebus which pierced the serpent Python" (Ibid).

The Sun was regarded as the father of Astral Light and the moon its mother.

The Light emanates from the Sun and receives form and rhythmic movement from the influence of the Moon, while the atmosphere is its receptacle and prison.

"The earth is the nurse," -- that is to say, it is equilibrated and motivated by the internal heat of the earth. "It is the universal principle, the Telesma of the world."

Hermes explained in what manner Astral Light, which is also a force, can be applied as a lever, as a universal dissolvent, and as a formative and coagulative agent; how also Astral Light must be extracted from the bodies in which it lies latent in order to imitate all the artifices of natural phenomena by the aid of its diverse manifestations as fire, motion, radiant gas, scalding water, and finally igneous earth.

According to legend, the Emerald Tablet was found by Alexander the Great in the tomb of Hermes, where it was hidden by the Masters of Egypt in the depths of the Great Pyramid. It was supposed to have been written by Hermes on a large plate of emerald by means of a pointed diamond (p. 79).

The old astronomers dedicated the Emerald to Mercury; and Berthelot says that this was in conformity with the ideas of the Egyptian Masters, who classed the Emerald and Sapphire in their list of metals.

The planet Mercury was the planet of Hermes, and it may be that some mythical connection was believed to exist between quicksilver and the precious stone.

Certain other works attributed to Hermes, such as the Divine Pymander, Asclepius, Minerva of the World, etc., are generally regarded as productions of the Alexandrian School. But they contain the Hermetic traditions which were preserved in theurgic sanctuaries.

The doctrines of Hermes can never be lost for those who possess the keys of the symbolism.

Amidst all their ruins, wrought chiefly by the Mother Church, the monuments of Egypt are as so many scattered leaves which can be collected and the book of those doctrines thus reconstructed entirely. In that vast book, the capital letters are temples and the sentences are cities, punctuated with the obelisks and the sphinx.

The reader will be surprised to learn that the physical division of Egypt was itself a magical synthesis, and the names of its provinces corresponded to the ciphers of the sacred numbers.

The realm of Sesostris was divided into three parts. Of these, Upper Egypt, of the Thebaid, was a type of the celestial world and the land of ecstasy. Lower Egypt was the symbol of the earth. Middle or Central Egypt was the land of science and of the high initiation.

And each of these divisions was subdivided into ten provinces, called Nomes, and was placed under the particular protection of a god.

This made thirty gods, and they were grouped by threes, giving symbolical expression in this manner to all possible conceptions of the Triad within the Decad, or otherwise, to the threefold material, philosophical and religious significances of absolute ideas attached primitively to numbers.

We thus have the first triangle of Unity, or the Number 1. The second triad corresponds to the duad, or Number 2, and its reflection is the Six-pointed Star of Solomon; the triple triad, or the complete idea under each of its three forms; the triple quaternary, being the cyclic number of astral revolutions, and so onward.

The geography of Egypt under Sesostris was therefore a pentacle or symbolical summary of the entire magical dogma originating with Zoroaster and rediscovered or formulated more precisely by Hermes.

In this manner, Egypt itself was a great volume or a scroll, and the instructions contained therein were multiplied by translation into pictures, sculptures, architecture through the length and breadth of the towns and in all the temples.

The very desert had its eternal teachings, and its word of stone was set squarely on the foundations of the pyramids.

The pyramids themselves stood like boundaries of the human intellectuality, in the presence of which the colossal Sphinx meditated age after age, being buried up by insensible degrees in the desert sand, until it and the Great Pyramid were almost completely buried when the earliest Egyptians settled in the Nile Valley, says Hotema in "The Mysterious Sphinx."

Even in this day, its face, badly scarred by the bigoted priesthood of the Mother Church, still emerges from its sepulchre, as waiting expectantly the signal for its complete entombment at the coming of a human voice revealing to a new world the secret of the pyramids.

From our standpoint, Egypt is the cradle of science and wisdom, for it clothed with images the antique dogma of the first Zoroaster more exactly and more purely, if not more richly, than those of India.

The Sacerdotal Art and the Royal Art made adepts by initiation in Egypt, and such initiation was not restricted within the egotistic limits of caste.

A Jewish bondsman himself attained not only initiation, but the rank of minister-in-chief, perhaps even of Grand Hierophant. For he espoused the daughter of an Egyptian priest, and there is evidence that the priesthood in that country tolerated no misalliance.

In Egypt, Joseph realized the dream of communion. He established the priesthood and the state as sole proprietors, and thus sole arbiters of labor and wealth. In this way he abolished economic distress and transformed the whole of Egypt into a patriarchal family.

It is a matter of historical knowledge that Joseph's elevation was due to his skill in the interpretation of dreams, -- an ancient science which even devout Christians now refuse to credit; yet they believe that the Bible, which narrates the wonderful divinations of Joseph, is the "Word of God." Just more Christian inconsistency.

The science of Joseph was that of the Chaldean Astrologers, and was based on a comprehension of the natural analogies which subsist between the ideas and the images, or between the Word (J H V H) and its symbols.

Joseph had been taught that when the Ego is immersed by sleep in the Astral Light, it perceives the reflection of its most secret thoughts and even of its presentiments. And he knew that the art of translating the Hieroglyphics of sleep is the key of universal lucidity, seeing that all intelligent beings have strange revelations in dreams.

The basis of absolute hieroglyphical science was an alphabet in which cosmic principles were represented by letters, letters represented ideas, ideas were convertible into numbers, and numbers were perfect signs. Such was the Hebrew alphabet, based on the hieroglyphical science of the Egyptians.

This hieroglyphical alphabet, thus originated, was the great secret which was enshrined in the Jewish Kabalah. It was originated in Egypt, and its Egyptian origin is commemorated in the Sepher Yetzirah, in which it is referred to Abraham.

Now, this Hebrew alphabet of 22 letters was formulated from the famous Book of Thoth, and it was divined by Count de Gebelin that it has been preserved to our own day in the form of the Tarot cards.

The record of the Tarot still exists among the drift and waste of Egyptian monuments and temples, demolished by the agents of the Mother Church.

Even today part of the figures of the Tarot can be seen in the ruins of the temples of Thebes, capitol of Egypt in 2000 B.C., and especially on an ancient ceiling of one of the halls of the palace of Midenit-Abou.

Its most curious, most complete key is found in the great work on Egypt by Athanasius Kircher. It is a copy of an Isiac tablet which belonged to the celebrated Cardinal Bembo.

This tablet is of copper with figures in enamel, and it has unfortunately been destroyed or concealed by the Mother Church.

Bembo divined that it contained the hieroglyphic key to the sacred alphabets, but he was unable to develop the explanation. It was divided into three equal compartments; above was the twelve houses of the astral realm, and below were the corresponding distributions of toil throughout the year, while in the middle place were the 21 sacred signs answering to the letters of the sacred alphabet.

In the midst, making 22 characters in all, was seated a figure of the pantamorphic IYNX, emblem of Universal Being or Universal Mind, and corresponding as such to the Hebrew Yod, or to that unique letter from which all other letters are formed.

The IYNX was encircled by the Ophite Triad, answering to the Three Mother Letters of the Egyptian and Hebrew alphabets.

On the right were the ibimorphic and serapin triads; on the left were those of Nepthys and Hecate, representing the active and passive elements, fixed and volatile, fructifying Fire and generating Water, -- two of the Four Elements.

Each pair of triads in conjunction with the center produces a septenary, and a septenary is contained in the center.

The three septenaries furnished the absolute number of the three worlds, the aerial, fluidal and physical, as well as the complete number of primitive letters, to which a complementary sign was added, like zero to the nine numerals.

The ten numbers and the 22 letters were termed in Kabalism the 32 Paths of Wisdom, and their philosophical description was the subject of the venerated primeval book, the Sepher Yetzirah.

According to the Astrologers, the universe developed into differentiated existence in conformity with the law of numbers. Ten emanations from the Cosmic Center manifest on every plane as 3 general and 7 specific attributes.

In their interaction with one another they form, by a principle similar to that giving musical overtones, 22 less abstract and more specialized influences, or astrological qualities.

These, manifesting as the 12 zodiakol signs and 10 planets of the chain, together with the 10 original numbers, form the 32 Paths of Wisdom, which are really the 32 factors of all manifested existence.

Yet, at any given time, all these 32 influences converge at every point in the universe. That is, in some Quantity they are everywhere present. And the specific point where they thus manifest -- the earth, for instance -- being a synthesis of their influence, constitutes a 33rd factor.

The Hebrew alphabet was divided into (1) Three Mother Letters, Aleph, Mem and Shin; (2) Seven Double Letters, Beth, Gimel, Daleth, Kaph, Pe, Resh, Tau; and (3) Twelve Simple Letters, He, Vau, Zain, Beth, Teth, Yod, Lamed, Nun, Samech, Ayin, Tsade, Quoph.

The oracles of the Tarot give answers as exact as mathematics and as measured as the harmonies of Nature. Such answers result from the varied combinations of the different symbols.

According to the Bible, the Israelites, led by Moses, carried off the sacred vessels of the Egyptians when they left the land of "bondage".

The account is entirely allegorical. The sacred vessels represented the mysteries of Egyptian wisdom, which were acquired by Moses himself at the court of Pharaoh.

The Hebrews got their education from the Chaldeans and the Egyptians, and the Hebrew scriptures are modified versions of the writings of those from whom they received their edification.

Chapter V

SWINDLE OF MYTHOLOGISM

Not many in the Christian world have yet gotten their eyes opened sufficiently to see, that the Holy Bible is a clever compilation of ancient fables and dramas, compiled from scrolls prepared by master dramatists and poets.

It was all a base plot, conceived by clever men and indirectly finan-
ced by the Roman tax-payers.

In the 4th century A.D. a group of crafty bishops persuaded Constantine
the Great to believe it was possible to rule the religious life of his people as well as their political life. He craved more power, and their argu-
ments easily convinced him that it could be done.

So, the bishops compiled a book from the ancient scrolls, called it the
infallible "Word of God," and used it to scare the people and rule the nation.

The trick was a booming success, but exceedingly costly. It required
the slaughter of more than seventy million people, produced the fall of the
Roman Empire, and ushered in a period of intellectual darkness that lasted
for more than a thousand years.

In the last century unprejudiced investigators have unearthed overwhelming evidence to prove that the Bible is a book of --

       1. Fables factualized   3. Symbols personalized
       2. Allegories literalized   4. Drama historicalized.

First of all, to ascribe the biblical books to any certain set of authors, as the makers of the Bible did, is to trespass on the ground of sheer
folly and base falsehood.

In the common sense of the term, the books of the Bible were never
"written" at all. No set of men ever sat down and composed them out of their
thoughts, observations, experiences, and knowledge.

What the ancient scrolls actually contained were the outlines of ancient tradition and legend, formulated by the accumulated wisdom of ancient
sages, covering the observations and experiences of mankind for hundreds of
thousands of years.

Out of that wisdom there came forth those set formulations of cosmic data,
cosmic laws, and moral codes that have survived the test of time, and still
stand as scientific committments.

For that accumulated wisdom presents in fable,, fiction, parable, allegory, symbol and dramatic poetry, the substantial facts of life, collected
and correlated by ancient sages.

And, furthermore, the work in its entirety is so profound, that sixteen
hundred years of the most consecrated effort of modern men to fathom it, has
left its esoteric meaning still unrevealed.

But the time of increasing knowledge has come when persistent workers
and unprejudiced investigators are slowly tearing the deceptive mask of literary disguise from the face of the ancient scriptures.

And it comes as a startling surprise for one to discover, that what has
been gratuitously assumed to be the product of primitive naivete and heathenish superstition, is now seen to be the variegated cloak of a recondite
wisdom.

Not only do the strange symbols and ridiculous allegories bear the im-
press of genius competent to portray cosmic facts in comic figures and ludri-

crous fables, but these ancient authors register an equal skill in their art-
ful concealment.

The employment by the sages of the crafty disguise, has carried them so
far beyond us in knowledge and skill, that we have been gulled into accepting
the disguise for the real thing. Well, that is, under the persuasion of the
priesthood, with the bitter alternative of burning for doubting.

By the dawning light of a better day we begin to see that the authors of
the ancient scrolls were master dramatists and clever poets.

The scrolls were first prepared as dramatic poetry; and the changing of
the Bible from poetry to prose was not completed until the 14th century. That
is additional evidence to prove what the Bible really is.

With soft touches and deft strokes did the ancient sages weave their profound pattern of terrenic life, of astral powers and physical phenomena, thru
their clever narratives of gods, men, mermaids, harpies, satyrs, centaurs,
sphinxes, serpents, stags, dragons, boars, bulls, of labyrinths, mountains,
seas, rivers, whirlwinds, clouds of fire and falling stars, that not the most
outlandish detail of their fabrications can be ignored, without the loss of
some signal link of meaning.

Generations of scholars, chained for a thousand years in the cave of
theological darkness, have perennially scoffed the suggestion that the ancient myths might be fanciful portrayals of esoteric facts.

And these scholars of darkness have charged the Chaldeans, Egyptians and
Greeks, the most enlightened races known in history, with possessing the ment-
ality of immature children.

We have accused them of taking their three-headed dogs, fire-breathing
dragons, beasts with seven heads and ten horns, their griffins, naiads, Cy-
clops, Circes, and Medusas, for definite actualities.

ANCIENT WISDOM

A New Age is approaching which will witness a most significant event --
the Renaissance of the Ancient Wisdom.

Intelligent people are forced to realize that Christianity has long been
discredited. It has failed to improve the condition of humanity, and is
threatened with obliteration by rampant forces that are hostile to its fraudulent claims.

Since Communism swept it overboard in Russia in 1917, the Church, in
self-defense, has called Communists all those who have denounced its theology
for what it is -- pure hogwash and hokum.

And since the churches in Russia were closed and replaced with schools
of learning, that nation has made more progress in forty years than the
Christian countries have made in four hundred years.

The superior knowledge vouchsafed from early graduates in the Cosmic
School of Life to disciplined pupils of the Ancient Mysteries of old, was
transmitted for ages and ages from generation to generation by oral teaching,
and concealed from the eyes of the world in scrolls of symbology and allegory.

Overwhelming evidence indicates that the taking of the ancient ritual dreams and scriptural myths for objective history, and the symbolical figures for real persons, has been the fountain source of the most abject corruption of human intellect since the beginning of the world.

While mechanical exploitations in this age have been marvelous, religion and philosophy have sunk to the very lowest levels.

The two chief causes responsible for this are: (1) Physical science has ignored the astral nature and motivation of the universe, and (2) ecclesiasticla zealotry, blinded by bigotry, has rendered religion ridiculous.

At this moment, the common intellectuality of the day, guided by a science based on materialism, and led and fed by a compactly institutionalized ecclesiastical power, stands committed in ideas as to the origin, structure, meaning and destiny of man, which are the lowest in all the history of the race.

ons in theology bearing upon the basic realities of man's relation to the universe are presented in pulpits, Sunday schools, and theological seminaries which the uncorrupted, natural intelligence of an eight-year-old child shrinks from in terror, or accepts with gloomy dismay.

Philosophy and religion are propagated on the basis of a theology that is received by the masses without comprehension, entirely repudiated by the intelligentsia, and brazenly dissembled by the very priesthood that lips its canto and its oracles from Sunday to Sunday.

To begin with, the biblical makers fraudulently changed symbols to real personages and allegory to factual history, and then centuries of erroneous indoctrination have so warped the intelligence and victimized the mind of the masses, that efforts to reach them with facts and truths are almost fruitless.

Biblical material presented as history and accepted as such is the variest nonsense.

The Freethinkers have been highly successful in disproving it as history. But they lack the basic knowledge of life to redeem it for what it actually is. Being guided by the postulate of evolution, they can not rise above the level of their belief; nor should one expect them to do so.

The fables and allegories of the Bible, as historical events, never happened. Nor was it ever imagined by their original authors that anyone could be so stupid and depraved as to believe them as realities.

They were originally designed to conceal the facts of life from the eyes of the world, and were used in the Ancient Mysteries to teach the neophyte the mystery of Man.

ANCIENT MASTERS

It will shatter current orthodoxy in science and philosophy to present the truth and establish the fact that archaic man possessed supernal sapiency.

It will be a surprise for many to learn that out of the night of remote antiquity there looms the Glorious Light of a transcendent intelligence on the part of numerous sages and seers.

The cradle of humanity, according to some scholars, was the sunken continent of Lemuria, and from there, we are told, came the Philosophy of Fire which the biblical makers strove so diligently to eliminate from the record as they compiled their Bible from the ancient scrolls.

In spite of their cautious work, many traces appear in the Bible to show that the Living Fire was the God of the Hebrews (Heb. 12:29).

At a period so remote as to be contemporary with the times incorrigibly marked by historians as "primitive," the Ancient Masters possessed scrolls of such exalted Astral Light and Intellectual Content as to lie beyond the comprehension of vaunted modern intelligence.

The time has come when modern pride must face the fact that these "primitive" people possessed scrolls which, by no possibility, could have been the product of "primitive" intellectuality.

Ancient scrolls which only ancient sages could have produced, bespeak the presence of sages on the scene. For men are known by their fruits.

The presence of sapient writings, the evidence of lost arts, the crumbling remains of edifices surpassing all present achievements -- these things attest incontrovertibly to the existence of Intellectual Giants in "primitive" times.

Further proof of this is found in the fact that prehistoric lore teems with accounts of a Golden Age, of heroes and giants of divine stature, of demigods, and sons of God who mingled with men, and left codes of laws and manuals of civilization which manifest a mastery not possible of acquirement by "primitive" people, and not yet achieved by modern man.

The names of some of these appear as Hermes, Buddha, Zoroaster, Osiris, Orpheus, Cadmus, Laotse, Hammurabi, while hundreds of others hover in the dim light of remote legendary days, as figures transcending by far what we consider normal human stature, and leaving behind as evidence of their greatness, those scrolls which have held up, thru the ages, as the norm of perfect wisdom and spotless conduct.

By a group of scheming men, beginning in the 4th century, the Bible was finally compiled from their writings, which consisted of fables, fiction, parables, allegories and symbols, and then presented to a deceived world as the infallible "Word Of God."

Then, to hide the facts, the ancient scrolls were destroyed.

FACTS IN FABULOUS FORM

Modern science admits that it is incompetent to explain the nature of Life or to analyze the constitution of Man.. The fact is attested by two leading scientists.

The great Dr. Alexis Carrel said: "Our knowledge of the human body is, in truth, most rudimentary. It is impossible, for the moment, to grasp its constitution" (Man The Unknown, 1935, p. 109).

The renowned Dr. Robert A. Millikan wrote: "I cannot explain why I am alive rather than dead. Physiologists can tell me much about the mechanical and chemical processes of my body, but they cannot say why I am alive." (Collier's, Oct. 24, 1925).

The Ancient Masters considered the substance and not the shadow. They looked not at the things which are seen, but at the things which are not seen. For the things seen are temporal, but the things not seen are eternal.

The Masters discerned the real figure thru the fog. They saw Man as a cosmic compound of four segments or strata of substance, possessing what may be termed four interpenetrated bodies, expressing phases ranging from the dense physical coarseness thru the various gradients of astral tenuity, each finer phase interpenetrating successively its coarser substrata, and being bound in linkage by the cosmic force of Polarity Affinity, as Hotema has explained in "The Flame Divine."

The deeper lore of remote antiquity dealt with a keen analysis of substance, the formulation of laws of action between the several phases in man, and catalogued the extensive schedule of these activities of consciousness in that amplified psychology of the sages, to a degree of perfection that to us appears astounding.

The science of psychology of the sages contains names for a host of sharply drawn segmentations of subjective activity which all modern probing has never systematically distinguished.

The gods of the sages were not ghostly shadows, but cosmic forces appearing on earth in the form of Life and Mind, — realities of the cosmos, and by no means the fanciful nonentities which have befogged the preachers and befuddled the laity thru the centuries.

These "gods" were the personified rays and energies of the universe, which modern science is only now beginning to discover, and going hog-wild over the greatness of the discoveries.

When we are competent to comprehend it, we can see that the knowledge of the Masters shows that man may step up from the status of a victim of evolution's forces that results from ignorance of the law, into the ranks of the sage who works harmoniously with the cosmic plan.

But that higher level, we regret to say, lies beyond the attainment of the masses at large, as long as they are controlled by institutions that live on darkness and thrive on ignorance.

And how can the controlled masses ever be lifted up from their low level? For the facts of history show how easily ecclesiastical propaganda has, more than once, produced mass-psychological-hysteria that is extremely dangerous for unorthodox teachers, as witness the terrible work of the Crusades and the Inquisition.

He who has the knowledge and the courage to attempt to improve the lot of the masses, would be murdered by them before he could finish the first lesson of life.

And these same deceived and enslaved masses ask the silly question, "Why do the Masters not come out in public and teach us the ways of life?"

Make safe and straight the way of
the Masters, and they will appear.

Chapter VI

THE TAROT

In preparing this work covering the
Tarot Symbolism, the author consulted
the works of the leading commentators
on the subject, including those of Eli-
phas Levi, Dr. A. E. Waite, Dr. F. H.
Curtiss, Manly P. Hall, Prof. P. D.
Ouspensky, Carl O. Huni, C. C. Zain,
Andrew Thomas, Paul F. Case and Frank
Lind.

A true and correct decipherment of
the Tarot Symbolism must conform to the
principles of the Ageless Wisdom of the
Ancient Masters as preserved in the
symbology and allegory contained in the
Christian Bible and in other ancient
scriptures, otherwise the interpretation
will fail to agree with the teachings
of the Masters who originated and designed the Major Arcana.

In his "Key To The Tarot," Dr. E.
E. Waite wrote:

"The true Tarot is symbolism. It
speaks no other language and offers no
other signs. Given the inward meaning
of its emblems, they do become a kind
of alphabet which is capable of indefinite combinations and makes true sense
in all.

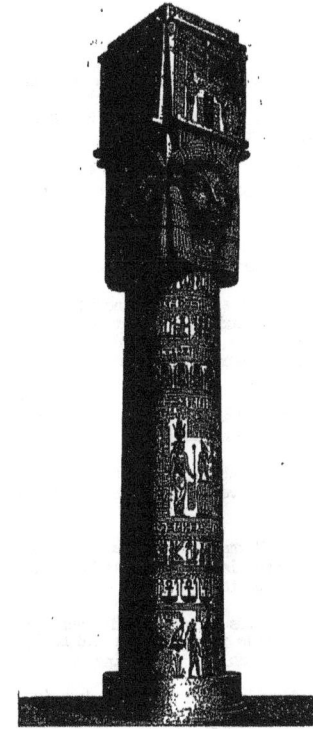

"On the highest plane it offers a key to the (Ancient) Mysteries, in a
manner which is not arbitrary and has not been read in. But the wrong symbolical stories have been told concerning it, and the wrong history has been
given in every published work which so far has dealt with the subject.

"It has been intimated by two or three writers that, at least in respect
of the meanings, this is unavoidably the case, because few are acquainted
with them, while these few hold by transmission under pledges and cannot be-
tray their trust.

"The suggestion is fantastic on the surface, for there seems a certain
anti-climax in the proposition that a particular interpretation of fortune-

telling -- l'art le tirer les cartes -- can be reserved for Sons of the Doctrine.

"The fact remains, however, that a Secret Tradition exists regarding the Tarot, and as there is always the possibility that some minor arcana of the Mysteries may be made public with a flourish of trumpets, it will be as well to go before the event and to warn those who are curious in such matters, that any revelation will contain only a third-part of the earth and sea and a third-part of the stars of heaven in respect of the symbolism.

"This is for the simple reason that neither in root-matter nor in development has more been put into writings, so that much will remain to be said after any pretended unveiling.

"The guardians of certain Temples of Initiation who keep watch over the mysteries of this order, have therefore no cause for alarm."

With respect to the interpretation of the Tarot symbolism, another commentator, in referring to the mind-controlled multitude, said that beyond a certain limit, he who knows would speak to no purpose, as he would not be understood. "The revelation of the Great Magical Secret of the Ancient Masters is therefore happily impossible."

"The Tarot is the most ancient of (all) books," wrote Dr. F. H. Curtiss in "The Key To The Universe," published in 1917, and he added:

"It is a collection of cards embodying the Secret Doctrine of the ages, almost every (ancient) nation having its version or variation of this synthetic exposition of the Ancient Wisdom.

"The Egyptian version is called The Book of Hermes; the Hebrew, The Book of Adam; while the version which we shall interpret is the one best known to the Western World, the Bohemian Tarot, or 'Bible of the Gypsies.'"

"The Gypsie Bible is composed of a deck of cards upon which the Ancient Wisdom is expressed in symbols, but like all symbols that are true and basic, they reveal their meaning only to those who are capable of receiving it.

"In many respects it is the Key which will unlock the mythical doctrines and philosophies of the Old World, and is called the Arcana of the Clavicles of Solomon.

"It is symbolized by a Key whose head is a ring composed of a circle containing the Four Cardinal Signs (of the Zodiakos), the Bull, the Lion, the Eagle and the Angel; its trunk or body bearing the 22 characters, and having the three degrees of the triad for its wards. It is sometimes called 'The Key of things kept secret from the foundation of the world' ".

The earliest historical reference to the Tarot in modern times was made in Europe in 1299.

Some commentators think the Tarot reached Europe with the first caravans of Gypsies. But they did not arrive in Western Europe until about 1400, and the Tarot was then already known.

And who were the Gypsies? They were Egyptians and called themselves Egyptians, but the Europeans thought they said "Gypsies."

Other commentators assert that the Tarot was brought from the East by the Crusaders, and it appears very probably that the Crusades were instrumental in planting the cards on European soil, just as the Arabic numerals, Algebra and other useful things were imported from Arabia by the returning soldiers of Christendom.

It is a significant fact that the appearance of the Tarot in Europe between 1300 and 1322 coincides with the prosecution of the Knights-Templar by Philip the Fair of France and Pope Clement V, and the ultimate burning of their Grand Master De Molay in 1314, as related by Hotema in "Cosmic Creation."

Carl O. Huni wrote that, according to tradition, the Tarot cards are the pages of the Book of Thoth which was saved by the Hierophants of Serapis at the time of the burning of the Alexandrian library. He said:

"Even today part of the figures of the Tarot can be seen in the ruins of the temples of Thebes, capitol of Egypt in 200 B.C., and especially on an ancient ceiling of one of the halls of the palace of Midniet-Abou.

"The Book of Thoth, also called Hermes Trismegistus, is the only document which contained the original teachings of the Tarot symbolism, and which was about the only thing saved when the priceless Egyptian library was burned" (The Tarot).

The Tarot consists of four suits of cards, and the oldest names of the suits in Italian were Deneri, Coppe, Bastoni, and Spade - or Coins, Cups, Batons and Swords.

The ancient Hindu goddess Ardhanari holds in her four hands a Ring, a Cup, a Wand, and a Sword, or the exact replicas of the four suits of the Tarot which represent the Four Elements, Fire, Air, Water and Earth.

According to Anaximander (611 - 545 B.C.), in the creative process, (1) Fire is the primal element, and gives birth to the other three as stated by Hotema in "Cosmic Creation."

Fire produces gases which form the element called (2) Air, which becomes (3) Water when the temperature falls, and Water, slowly coagulating forms all solid matter which constitutes the (4) Earth.

Thus did the ancients explain in a few words the mystery of Creation, which is a perpetual process, without beginning and without ending, and needs the aid of no church God.

All the evidence indicates that the Tarot had a very ancient origin. But all traces of it were so utterly destroyed by the Church Fathers to conceal the central doctrine of the ancient philosophy, that it was entirely unknown in the Western World until the 14th century.

The Tarot of the Bohemians by Dr. Gerard Encausse, who wrote under the pseudonym of Papus, and a translation of which was edited by Dr. Arthur E. Waite, is the work best known to the Western World, as stated above, and contains an interesting story concerning the Egyptian Tarot as follows:

"A time followed when Egypt, no longer able to struggle against her invaders, prepared to die honorably.

"Then the Egyptian savants held a great assembly to arrange as to how the knowledge, which until then had been confined to men judged worthy to receive it, should be saved from oblivion.

"At first they thought of confiding these secrets to virtuous men secretly recruited by the Initiates themselves, who would transmit them from generation to generation.

"But one of the Masters, observing that virtue is a most fragile flower and the most difficult to find, at all events, in a continuous line, proposed to confide the scientific traditions to vice.

"The latter, said he, would never fail completely and thru it we are sure of a long and durable preservation of our principles.

"This opinion evidently prevailed, and the game chosen as a vice was preferred.

"The small plates were then engraved with the mysterious figures which taught the most important scientific secrets of the Masters, and since then the players of cards have transmitted this Tarot from generation to generation far better than the most virtuous men upon the earth would have done, and at the same time have been utterly ignorant of the meaning of the symbolism."

Papus wrote two books devoted to the Tarot; but he lived in the Dark Ages when the rank and file of the masses knew nothing except what was taught by the church, and at a time when it was dangerous to teach anything not sanctioned by the church. So, the result was that the Ancient Wisdom concealed in the mysterious cryptograms mostly "went over his head."

All works on the Tarot contain something of interest, but they also contain much hogwash and hokum, which is characteristic of all "occult" literature in general.

There is first a purely scholastic search for the meaning of the letter, second, too hasty conclusions, covering with platitudinous ponderosity that which is unintelligible to the author himself, the ignoring of difficult questions, unfinished speculations, and third, unnecessary complexity and unsymmetrical construction.

The books of Papus on the Tarot, who in his day was the most popular commentator on the cryptograms, are especially rich in this thrasonical bombast.

Papus himself admits that all complexity indicates the imperfection of a system. And that certainly applies 100% as to medical art and Christianity. He said:

"Nature is very synthetic in her manifestations, and simplicity lies at the base of her most intricate phenomena."

He knows not what Nature is. Nature is the phenomenal world, the work and product of Cosmic Creation. Nature does nothing. Nature is.

But Papus is correct as to the simplicity of Cosmic Creation, and precisely is this simplicity lacking in all expositions of the Tarot.

The authors who have written about the Tarot have exalted this system to the sky, calling it the Universal Key, but they have certainly lacked the knowledge and ability to demonstrate how this Key should be used.

One of these, and perhaps the greatest, was Eliphas Levi, who wrote:

"An imprisoned person, with no other book than the Tarot, if he knew how to use it, could in a few years acquire universal knowledge and would be able to speak on all subjects with unequalled learning and inexhaustible eloquence" (Transcendental Magic).

Levi went a little too far. If he actually knew that much about the symbolism of the Tarot, he failed to present the knowledge in his own work.

The true Tarot consisted of 78 picture cards, but now the term Tarot is applied only to the 22 Major Arcana. And it is these to which this work is devoted.

The word TAROT literally means a wheel or something that rotates. The Ancient Masters recognized the secret of the Cosmic Cycle. In the Jarvis Letters it is stated:

"The importance of the picture of the Orb which named all wheels, is further shown in the fact that human language was made on this Ball, Circle, Wheel. Thus ORB-IT names 'the going of the Orb', and even the rut in the road made by the wheel is called 'Orbita', because the rut shows the route, rute, ruis or way, or road of the Wheel.

"Any schoolboy can understand the general plan for the making of words on the Sun. The Rota or Wheel named everything Rotary and going in rota-tion, and that which was attributed to the action or causings of the Sun, such as rolling, roting, roasting."

The five letters of the word Tarot encircle the very ancient Solar Cross of Life, formed in Astrology by the Four Fixed Signs of the Zodiakos; Aries, Cancer, Libra, and Capricorn; which represent the Four Elements symbolized by the Sphinx - Fire, Air, Water, and Earth, and which constitute the Fourfold Basis of Cosmic Creation, as explained by Hotema.

Moving clockwise, "T" is over Aries, head sign of the Zodiakos; "A" is the point of the right arm of the Solar Cross, Capricorn; "R" is the point at the bottom of the verticle beam of the Cross, Libra; "O" is the point at the left arm of the Cross, Cancer; and "T" is repeated at the top of the Cross, over Aries, the starting point.

From the Tarot has been drawn the inspiration for some of the most important works of Occult Wisdom published in the last hundred years.

Many intelligent authors of mystical books have modeled their works on the plan of the Tarot; but usually their readers, knowing nothing of the Tarot, never even suspect this, as the Tarot is generally not mentioned. If it were, the average layman would not know what it is.

The revival of interest in the Tarot began about a century ago with the writings of Alphonse Louis Constant, under the pseudonym of Eliphas Levi; but as he was a Roman Catholic and believed the Church was born just in time to save civilization, the Ageless Wisdom preserved in the symbolism of the Tarot also "went over his head."

Levi said that the Tarot was his most valuable source of information, and his writings had great influence on the mind of Helena P. Blavatsky, the Founder of Theosophy.

The Ancient Masters arranged the Tarot in three parts:

       1st part - 21 cards numbered 1 to 21;
       2nd part - one card numbered 0.
       3rd part - 56 cards of four suits of 14 cards in each suit.

The cards numbered from 0 to 21 deal with the Greater Arcana, and are called Trumpa Major.

These are the 22 cards which the Church Fathers had in their possession when they compiled their Bible, and then destroyed the cards so completely that no traces of them can be found anywhere, except as we have stated above.

These are the 22 cards which form the important part of the Tarot, and are the ones in which we are interested.

And why were they thus destroyed? For the same reason that the ancient libraries were burned and the ancient scrolls destroyed. They revealed too much of the Ageless Wisdom which the Church has tried so hard for sixteen hundred years to keep from seeing the light of day.

One of the best works on the Tarot was written by P. Christian. In his History of Magic he described the ritual of initiation into the Egyptian Mysteries in which a leading role was played by the pictures of the 22 missing Arcana of the Tarot. This is what he said:

"The neophyte enters a long gallery, supported by caryatides in the form of 24 sphinxes, 12 on each side. On each part of the wall between the sphinxes there were frescoed paintings, representing the mystical figures and symbols (of the greater Arcana). These 22 pictures faced one another in pairs. ... (These pairs we have listed below).

"As the neophyte was escorted past the 22 pictures of the gallery, he received appropriate instruction from his conductor, consisting of an interpretation of the symbolism.

"Each arcanum, made visible and tangible by each of these 22 pictures, is a formula of the law of human activity in its relation to astral and physical forces, the combination of which produces the phenomena called Life."

It is important to observe that, according to these statements, gods and saviors were not involved. The symbolism of the 22 Trumpa Major dealt with the Law of Life, and with all related phenomena.

We have repeatedly stated in our various works which Resurrect the Ageless Wisdom of the Ancient Masters, that it would destroy the sordid institutions of the earth, which live on ignorance and thrive on darkness, if man were taught correctly the secret of Life and the constitution of his own body, the Temple of the Living God, which God man himself is, as stated by Paul in the Bible (1 Cor. 3:16).

Of the many authors we consulted on the Tarot, Ouspensky is the only one who discovered that it is feasible to arrange the Major Arcana in certain pairs, as they evidently were in the Egyptian Temple of Initiation, and establish a logical, sensible relation existing between them.

And here again, in this pairing, we meet another one of the regular tricks employed by the Masters to confuse the exoteric. Ouspensky paired the cards as follows:

1.	Magician	0.	Fool
2.	Priestess	21.	World
3.	Empress	20.	Resurrection
4.	Emperor	19.	Sun
5.	Hierophant	18.	Moon
6.	Temptation	17.	Star
7.	Chariot	16.	Tower
8.	Good	15.	Evil
9.	Hermit	14.	Time
10.	Wheel of Life	13.	Wheel of Death
11.	Justice	12.	Judgment

When arranged in pairs in this way, we shall see as we proceed that one card links in with the other and, what is most important, that they can thus be intelligently explained and understood only together, and not separately, for the symbolism of one card completes that of the other.

For instance, the first card, called the Juggler or Magician, represents Cosmic Elements and Creative Processes, called God by the Church; and its companion card, 0, the Fool, represents the newly incarnated Ego starting out in its unknown journey of terrestrial existence in a far country, and signifies the average man of darkness.

The second card, the High Priestess, represents the World Mother, Virgo, the Virgin of the skies, and variously called in different countries, Isis, Devaki, Mylitta, Astarte, Minerva, Ceroe, Mary, etc. And its companion card, 21, presents the World in the cycle of Time, the product of the Cosmic Elements and Creative Processes indicated in card one.

COSMIC CYCLE

It is well here to state that the Tarot Symbolism deals with and is founded upon the basic fact that Cosmic Creation is a steady, constant process, and moves in a continuous cycle.

Creation did not begin on a certain day or time, as stated in the Bible, and reach its finish and conclusion on a certain day or time, as stated in the Bible.

For Creation has no beginning and has no ending. It moves as a Wheel and Rotates as a Circle, with no beginning and no ending.

The simplest illustration that may be presented to demonstrate the Creative Cycle is that in the case of the element called water, whose symbolic color is Blue.

Even the man of darkness knows that water is condensed vapor, and becomes ice when the temperature falls low enough to produce the change. Then, as

Apocalyptic Key.
The Seven Seals of St John.

the temperature rises, the ice changes back to water, and a further rise in temperature causes the water to vaporize and disappear from sight.

Now, what has happened? Did the water and ice have a beginning and an ending? No. There was simply a transformation of elements under the Law of Creation.

But the man of darkness is not taught in the schools, colleges and medical institutions that the Creative Process pursues the same cyclic course in all instances, from water to man.

There is nothing mysterious about Creation when the basic principle is understood. Creation is Transformation, not beginnings and endings.

The same process operates in the vegetal, animal and humanal kingdoms. The only difference is in the nature and complexity of the objects created.

The mode of operation in the case of animals is more complicated, and, at the present stage of evolution, must be preceded by a definite act to set the creative process into operation, as explained by Hotema in "Cosmic Creation".

HEBREW ALPHABET

In his work, "History of Magic" Eliphas Levi said: "The alphabet of Thoth is the original of our Tarot only in an indirect manner, seeing that the latter is of Jewish origin in the extant copies and that its pictures are not older than the reign of Charles VII (p. 82).

Levi ignores the fact that the Tarot "of Jewish origin" was copied from the ancient Tarot of the Egyptians, the original of which no doubt came from Lemuria and Atlantis.

The Jews had the Tarot when they invented their alphabet of 22 letters it seems, and perhaps tried to make the letters fit the symbolism of the 22 Major Arcana, so some assert.

Frank Lind thinks the Jews failed in their attempt, and said:

"Astrologers, Alchemists, Kabbalists, Mystics, have all vied in trying to make the Tarot conform to their own system of belief. As Grillot de Givry rightly remarks, the agreement between the Hebrew alphabet and the cards of the Major Arcana does not go far" (How to Understand the Tarot, p. 16).

But Dr. Case and some others have assumed that the Jewish alphabet does conform to the Tarot symbolism, and so used it, beginning with Aleph, the first letter, and assigning it to card 0, The Fool. If this is erroneous,

then all thru his book Dr. Case has assigned the wrong Hebrew letters to the various cards.

Dr. H. F. Curtiss, in his "Key To The Universe", listed the first ten cards of the Major Arcana, omitting 0 and beginning with card 1. He assigned Aleph to card No. 1, the Magician, and said:

"The first letter of the Hebrew alphabet is Aleph, corresponding to our letter A, and its numerical value is 1. Like number 1, it expresses the out-breathing of the Divine or as the Kabbalah expresses it, 'soft breathing'. Aleph is the first of the mother letters, out of which all the others are produced. Also out of soft breathing are all the sounds expressed by the 22 letters" (p. 68).

It is well to give the reader something to make him do his own thinking, so we shall list the 22 letters of the Hebrew alphabet and he can make his own comparison between them and the 22 Major Arcana.

1. Aleph, a silent Hebrew letter denoting unity and commencement; to join together; to discipline. It symbllizes unity of atoms, of worlds; it represents the creative principle, the Ego, going forth into human embodiment.

2. Beth, meaning to build, to form, to create. Its radical meaning is a "house" or "birth-place". For instance, Beth-el is the "house of God"; Eliza-Beth, the "house of Eliza"; Beth-lehem, the "house of bread"; Bal-beth, the "house or temple of the sun".

3. Gimel, literally meaning a camel, and hieroglyphically meaning "a hand, half closed and extended in order to draw to its possessor that which is needed for his own sustenance". Three in the language of Hebrew principles stands for that which rules and directs, as the mind rules or directs the body.

In Aleph the Ego is incorporated in man as Adam; in Beth it finds its home or rest in the feminine Principle, Eve; and in Gimel we have the son or offspring.

4. Daleth, meaning a door to swing open and shut; completed action of cosmic generation. It is combined with the Sun (Card 16) and referred to fertility.

The Sun has a dual aspect in that while in its positive aspect it is the fructifying power which stimulates fertility, in its negative aspect it scorches, kills, produces putrefaction and causes the opposite of fertility, or sterility.

5. He, a window thru which light enters, to see, to behold, or in a deeper sense, stands for perception. It corresponds to the zodiakol sign Aries. It refers to humanity in some aspect, so the 5th letter He represents man as distinguished from all other animals.

While He is the Breath of Life which is shared by all animals, yet only man possesses the principle of Intelligence (Aries, the head) so well developed that he can use the breath to formulate and express his thoughts in intelligent speech.

While all animals have some form of intelligent communication, only man possesses the power of speech, the great gulf between man and all other animals which the hvolutionists have never been able to bridge.

6. Vau (V) meaning a peg, a hook, a conjunction, reciprocity and relation. The "6" is called hexad, from the Greek word hex, meaning 6, the Latin of which is sex. So, this is the house of suffering, or the house where the light mixes with darkness, or the Word (Ego) in the Flesh actively makes known its powers to mortal man.

7. Zain, meaning a scepter, sword, or weapon, while hieroglyphically it means an arrow, both meanings suggesting the idea of conquest.

At this stage in his life man must become a conqueror, with the kingly ability to rule first himself, then all nature, and with the power to defend, preserve and use the mystical weapon bestowed upon very Victor, namely, the Sword of the Ego, or the Fiery Sword of the Magician.

8. Heth, meaning fullness, a new cycle, a new sense. A new First as an octave in music, color, days of the week. Its hieroglyphic meaning is a cultivated field in which a crop is produced. It thus suggests labor and effort as well as the idea of increase and wealth.

The "field" is th- field of man's own nature and consciousness. Hence, the step indicated by the 8th letter should bring to man the increase of evolution. This can be attained only thru effort, battle, victory and balance and by sedulously cultivating the soil of his field.

9. Teth, a serpent, to twist or curve. As 9 is the Number of Initia-
t

tion, an Initiate is called a Naga or Serpent of Wisdom. Just as the serpen changes and renews its external skin, so the Initiate changes and renews his personality.

10. Yod, to praise, the origin of all things, for by and from Yod were all the other letters created. Its hieroglyph is "the finger of man," pointing upward, the sign of aspiration and also of command. Yod, representing the Active Principle of Life manifestations, symbolically stands for the Reincarnating Ego.

11. Kaph, to extend, to broaden; new hope or wish of the Ego in its involution toward matter or rebirth.

12. Lamed, signifying whiplash, to train, to teach. The number 12 signifies born in affliction and is kabbalistically associated with Benjamin,

12th son of Jacob.

The Zodiakos is symbolized in the word Jacob, which signifies an arch, a vault, a dome, which is set in order by cosmic processes, and then called Israel.

This dome or vault is the Zodiakos of the Heavenly Man or the arch or the curve of Heaven. It corresponds to the 12 faculties or lobes of the brain, and is likened to the offspring of Israel. The 12 sons of Jacob represent in reality the 12 faculties of the brain.

13. Mem, literally means "seas", water, to flow out.

14. Nun, a fish, to sprout, or life renewed thru form or manifestation.

15. Samekh, to uphold, to sustain or draw near, to refresh.

16. Ayin, a silent letter denoting prophecy; it intimates the superficial aspect of objects seen.

17. Pe, represents the Logos or Word.

18. Tsadhe, a hook or scythe, meaning to cut down, to reap.

19. Quoph, to encircle, to be quick or give instant recognition of things in the objective world.

20. Resh, the head or highest seat of Consciousness. It stands for intuition or the instant recognition and relation of things in the subjective world.

21. Schin, signifies a tooth, or to pierce, also engraftment.

22. Tau, denoting to grieve, repent or to abide. In the alphabet of principles it represents the crucifixion of the intersection of the horizontal line of involution by the vertical line of evolution.

S.S.S.

"Neither height nor depth can measure the possibilities of the human soul."

THE MAGICIAN.

THE FOOL.

Chapter VII

CARD 1, THE MAGICIAN & CARD 0, THE FOOL

Card 1, The Magician

Magus, Magician and Juggler are the various names given this card by the different commentators.

Magic is the ancient name of Science, especially the Hermetic Sciences.

We can think of nothing more magical than the creation of the flowers of the field and the beasts of the forest. And the same laws apply with equal force and effect to man, as shown by Hotema in "Cosmic Creation."

Card 1 presents the picture of a youthful figure, clad in the robe of a Magician. The figure has the bright countenance of Apollo, the Greek God of the Sun.

Above the head hovers a symbol of the Life Link, the Silver Cord mentioned in the Bible (Eccl. 12:6), which links together terrestrial and celestial Life, as Hotema explains in "The Flame Divine".

This symbol is to indicate the Macrocosmic character of the Magician. It signifies that he embodies the Creative Principle and personifies the

-52-

tetradic qualities of Life known as Consciousness, Mind, Intelligence and Vitality.

In short, the Magician represents that Universal Principle which the church calls God.

About his waist is a Serpent Cincture, the serpent appearing to swallow its tail, forming a Circle, the ancient symbol of Eternity.

In his left hand, pointing upward, is the Magic Wand, the serpent-wound Staff of Hermes, symbol of the Creative Power, Polarity, -- without which there would be no Creation, in spite of all the Gods invented by man.

His right hand points downward toward the earth, indicative of the ancient axiom, "As above, so below."

Before him stands a square table, representing the four hypothetical corners of the world. On the table are scattered the four symbols which represent the Four Great Elements of which the Universe is constituted, symbolized by the Sphinx in all nations of the ancient world.

This is the ancient secret of the Four Letters of the Ineffable Name, J H V H, which in turn, represent the Four Elements of Fire, Air, Water and Earth.

This fourfold elemental basis of Creation appears on each level of integration in a different guise, and is discussed in detail by Hotema in "Cosmic Creation".

These Four Great Symbols appear in a deck of common playing-cards, and are called Clubs, Hearts, Diamonds and Spades. By the ancients they were called Wands, Cups, Coins or Pentacles, and Swords. The two colors represent Polarity.

The Magician's sky-colored hat is symbolic of the Astral World. The lemniscate formed by its brim implies the orbit of the sidereal bodies.

The Great Magic

Creation is the Great Magic. The great mysteries of the Universe are the creative processes constantly occurring all around us; yet so trite and common to us that we never note nor reflect upon them. And science cannot explain them.

Take two small seeds, much alike, and let the chemist decompose them, analyze them, torture them in all the scientific ways he knows. The net result of each seed is a little sugar, a little fibrin, a little water -- carbon, potassium, sodium, and the like -- one cares not to know what, for to know can tell one nothing.

We plant the seeds in the ground. The rain moistens them, the sun shines on them, and little shoots spring up soon and grow. What a miracle.

One shoot develops into a slender, feeble stalk, soft of texture, like a common weed; the other a sturdy bush, of woody fiber, armed with thorns.

A miracle that no scientist can explain.

This is the creative work of the Four Great Elements of the Ancient Masters.

From (1) the earth, (2) the invisible air, (3) the limpid rain-water, and (4) solar fire, the chemistry of the seeds has extracted colors also -- shades of green that paint the leaves which put forth in the spring. Later come the flowers of various colors and odors.

A miracle that no scientist can explain. Is it a greater miracle to make Man?

One can think of nothing more mysterious and magical than the creation of the flowers of the field and the beasts of the forest.

The same cosmic laws apply to all things, including man.

And so, quite logically, Magic was the ancient name of Science; and the name of the first card was the Magician.

Card 0, The Fool

Some commentators place this card between Cards 20 and 21. It is the proper companion of card No. 1. Its symbolism, not understood by most of the commentators, deals chiefly with the Ego at the dawn of its incarnation.

Consider the youth of today. He is the Fool who, with light step as if the earth had no traps and trammels to worry him, pauses at the very brink of a sheer precipice among the heights of the world.

Clad in gay garments, his yellow hair bound by a green wreath, he calmly surveys the blue distance before him -- its expanse of sky rather than the prospects around him.

The deep precipice before him means nothing. It is as if angels were waiting to uphold him if he took another step that would plunge him into the deep abyss.

He appears as a Prince of another world, on his journey thru a far country (Lu. 15:13). The sun, shining behind him, knows whence he came, whither he is bound, and how he will return by another path after many days.

His inner garment, dazzling white, indicates purity. Dimly traced on its foldsaat the neck are the Four Symbols of the Ineffable Name, J. H. V. H., implying that he is the product of Fire, Air, Water, Earth.

His white vestment is almost entirely concealed by a black mantle, signifying darkness, and is lined with the red of passion that will drag him down.

He has The Mystic Rose in his left hand, which signifies Life, and his right hand balances a black rod over his right shoulder, from which there hangs at his back a wallet curiously embroidered, the flap of which is sown with ten stiches.

The lock of the flap forms a closed Eye, and below the flap is the picture of an eagle.

The rod represents power, by the use of which man brings into his Mind the manifestation of cosmic unity and completion, represented by the ten stiches on the wallet, and the ten circular ornaments on the Fool's black robe.

Ten is the number of Completion, of Perfection thru completion. It was a phallic number with the Jews. The eagle on the wallet, representing the zodiakol sign of Scorpio, was also a phallic emblem.

The 10th Sephira unfolds naturally from the 9th, and in the Number Ten completes the Cycle of The Mystic Rose, as well as the decad of the numbers.

The Mystic Rose in the Fool's left hand is white, indicating that freedom from the lower forms of Desire which produces the Hermit in Card 9. It is a cultivated flower, showing as do the other details of the Fool's vesture and equipment, that he comes from a world of cultural activity.

The Fool's robe is encircled at the waist by a girdle of twelve ornaments, of which seven are visible, signifying the Seven Incarnations thru which the Ego passes in its cycle.

These twelve ornaments represent the twelve signs of the Zodiakos, thru which are indicated the powers of the Astral Bodies as they affect man.

The icy mountain peaks in the background imply that the cold, abstract principles of Cosmic Law control terrestrial life.

The Closed Eye

The closed Eye on the wallet flap means so much that it merits especial attention.

In general, it signifies the closed Mind of the unthinking multitude.

We must remember that man is born into a world of rigidly standardized systems which stagnate his progress, stalemate his thinking, and stultify his Mind.

These systems permit no thinking and prevent mental development. They dormantize the brain.

The Mind is conditioned by controlled and standardized educational and theological systems. This conditioning process molds the Mind to fit the pattern prepared for it, and the pattern is cleverly designed to make man believe it elevates him when, in fact, it debases him.

So, the Eye on the Fool's wallet is "closed" to indicate this mental state.

Man's Mind "is the most colossal power in this world" wrote Dr. Carrel.

It can flash around the world in an instant, and span the future as well as the past.

The old man can see himself as a child playing with his toys, and the engineer can see the sky-scraper he plans to build, filled with people.

That phase of Ancient Wisdom appears in the Bible: --

We look not at the things seen with our eyes, but we look with our Mind at things not seen with our eyes. For the things seen with our eyes are temporal, while the things seen with our Mind and not seen with our eyes, are eternal (2 Cor. 4:18).

Nothing frightens those institutions that are founded on standardized systems so much as Thinking does. Because those who Think, usually find Truth and Light, -- two qualities entirely foreign to these institutions. So, the Thinking of the masses is done by these institutions.

The church did have the authority to murder and burn those who refused to accept its standardized line of thought, and exercised that authority freely and gaily for centuries.

Those stubborn, dangerous Thinkers were called "heretics." They were enemies of the church God, and the church, as God's terrestrial regent, had the "divine right" to destroy God's enemies.

The Mother Church declares: "Deciding for himself what he will believe, instead of accepting the (standardized) teachings of Christ and His Church, the heretic rejects truth and embraces error." This makes him an enemy of God and he thus forfeits his right to life.

That great writer Rupert Hughes said: "The thing that makes church members such 'Dangerous Citizens' is their (stupid) belief that they have a 'God' directing them, and that those who oppose them are 'opposing God'. This is the basic origin of all the horrors and holy wars."

It was not until 1816 that public pressure was so strong that it constrained the Pope to issue a bull putting "an end to torture and death (by burning) at the stake for opinion's sake (Wall, p. 341).

CREATION

Leading scientists declare that the Condition of the Earth is the Parent of Creation.

They cite the fact that no living thing can come into existence until the Condition of the Earth is perfectly suitable for living things to appear and survive.

That is the actual Law of Creation. Under that law man comes into existence. His creation, his appearance, is the proof that he was perfectly adapted to the conditions of the environment in which he appeared, as Hotema explains in his remarkable work, "Cosmic Creation."

That is a State of Perfection in which nothing is wanting and nothing is needed.

That ancient Doctrine of Perfection provided no place for the priesthood, and it made man the God of the physical world, as stated in the Bible (Gen. 1:26).

Then the time came when that Doctrine was debased and corrupted by the priesthood, and the Masters were silenced and slaughtered, and man was plunged into intellectual darkness.

And that is the Man of Darkness, symbolized by the Masters in the Tarot cartomancy as the Fool.

That man's Mind is closed. His thinking is done for him. He is taught from childhood to worship appearance and ceremonies, to believe in "sacred books" or the "writings of learned theologians," and to accept "the (standardized) teachings of (a mythical) Christ and His Church."

That man's Consciousness functions thru five faulty senses, and is extremely limited in its realization of the world in which that man lives.

That is the Fool, the Man of Darkness, who carries in a wallet the essence of the Knowledge which shold be his, but he knows it not. His ignorance of himself and of the world constrains him to stumble blindly on, constantly searching for that which he already has.

It is our purpose in this work to expose the fraudulent teachings of a mythical Christ and His Church which make man a Fool and keep him in intellectual darkness. And so, we shall meet the Fool frequently.

THE HIGH PRIESTESS

THE WORLD.

Chapter VIII

CARD 2, HIGH PRIESTESS & CARD 21, THE WORLD

Card 2, High Priestess

Card 2 presents, primarily, the Creative Principle, Polarity, Sexuality, Duality. It is the condition that develops naturally from the primal division of the Cosmic Unit, the fundamental phase of Creation.

This is not only a long story, but an important one, and the details of it are contained in Hotema's work titled "Cosmic Creation."

The High Priestess in this case is Isis, chief goddess of the Egyptian Mysteries. In this role she represented the World Mother, the Nurse of all Creation. Her priests were obligated to observe perpetual chastity, which placed them above the plane of animalistic propagation, the subject of the Edenic allegory.

In the picture Isis is crowned with the solar disk between two horns, indicative of the union of the positive and negative elements, which are further implied by the Solar Cross on her breast.

She sits between two pillars, one white and one black, representing the positive and negative properties of substance. These are also the two pillars of Masonry, Jachin and Boaz, and were prominently pictured at the entrance of Solomon's Temple.

"In magic," says C. C. Zain, this card "depicts the principle of reception, the polar opposite of the principle indicated in Arcanum 1. It is the feminine reaction of the magical agent, and teaches us the androgynous nature of Astral Light" (The Tarot, p. 93).

The bases of the pillars are cubes, representing the Four Elements, Fire, Air, Water, Earth. The capitals of the pillars represent Egyptian architecture, in the form of lotus buds, signifying creative action.

Isis sits at the entrance of the realm of Nature. The veil, extending between the pillars behind her, conceals the Mystery of Creation, and is not to be rudely lifted by the profane nor desecrated by the impious.

There is a scroll, or book, in her lap, or held in her right hand in some cards, on which is inscribed the word Tora, which is the phonetic equivalent of the Hebrew Torah, or "Law".

The various commentators have missed the point as to this scroll. One says it is to convey the message that the Scriptures have an esoteric meaning. Another says it is the Secret Law. Still another says it is the record of past events, of all mental and physical states, indelibly impressed in subconsciousness. All of them are wrong.

This book, in some sets of "Tarot Cards", also appears in Card 10, Wheel of Life, in which case the Four Creatures of Ezekiel occupy the angles of the cards, and each of them is reading the book.

This book is so important that Hotema dealt with it in detail in his "Son of Perfection," where he explains that it represents the Temple in which the Ego dwells (1 Cor. 3:16).

It is mentioned in the Bible as the Book With Seven Seals (Rev. 5). And little does the Christian world dream that the Seven Seals are actually Seven Great Nerve Centers of the human Temple.

These vital centers are called "seals" because in the man of darkness they are semi-dormant. This condition causes man's Consciousness to function on a very low level, exactly as desired by the Mother Church, and the result is that such a man lives in a very small world.

One purpose of initiation was to teach the Neophyte how to activate these Seven Major Batteries of the body, and thus greatly to expand the world in which he lived.

That was the path to Seership which the Church destroyed, and which we shall mention in our interpretation of Card 17, the Star, and also Card 9, the Hermit.

Of this book the Bible says:

"And I saw a strong angel proclaiming with a loud voice, Who is worthy to open the book, and to loose the seals thereof?

"And no man in heaven, nor in earth, neither under the earth, was able to open the book, neither to look therein.

"And I wept much, because no man was found worthy to open and to read the book, neither to look thereon.

"And one of the elders saith unto men, Weep not: behold, the Lion of the tribe of Judah, the Root of David, hath prevailed to open the book, and to loose the seals thereof" (Rev. 5:2-5).

The "strong angel" was Phannel, one of the four angels of the Solar God. The Lion is Leo, symbol of Solar Fire, and also the sign of Judah. The "root" of man is his Astral Self. For the mystical Tree of Life, Man, is the inverted ashvattha tree, which has its roots in the astral world and its branches in the physical world. Therefore, "the root of David" is David reincarnated.

"And I beheld, and lo, in the midst of the throne of the Four Beasts (symbols of Fire, Air, Water, Earth), and in the midst of the Ancients (symbols of the hours of the day), stood a Lamb, as if it had been sacrificed, having 7 horns and 7 eyes.

"And he came and took the book out of the hand of him seated on the throne (Rev. 5:6,7)."

The Lamb represents the trembling Neophyte, who has been prepared, tested and accepted for the ordeal of initiation in the Ancient Mysteries.

The horns and eyes represent the seven noetic powers of action and the seven noetic powers of perception, which are awakening in the body of the Neophyte.

A scholar who has read Yoga literature relating to the Kundalini and the Seven Chakras of man's body, knows where the last book of the Bible originated.

It was written by the Hindus thousands of years before the world ever heard of the gospel Jesus, and a copy of the scroll was brought back to Asia Minor by Apollonius about the middle of the first century A.D., when he visited India.

This Apollonius became the "Mystery Man of The Bible", the Jesus of the gospels, the Paul of the epistles, and the John of Revelation, as explained by Hotema in his various works.

When the "pious" Church Fathers copied the scroll for their Bible, they fraudulently changed the context to bring their mythical Jesus into the picture, and these interpolations are so conspicuous and produce such breaks in the narrative, that they can be sifted out by a highschool student.

This Jesus is the very foundation of Christianity, and it was imperative that he be mentioned in the Bible. That is the reason why the Bible was compiled by those who organized that religious system, and the only reason why the New Testament was written and added to the ancient literature.

When this Jesus was born, Christianity was born, and when he falls,
Christianity fails.

Initiation

Let us follow the Neophyte and see what occurs.

Being prepared, tested and accepted for initiation, the Neophyte was
ordered to enter the Great Pyramid during the night, and descend on hands
and knees thru a narrow passage without steps, until he reached a cavelike
opening, thru which he had to crawl to another subterranean cave, on the
walls of which were inscribed these words:

"The mortal who shall travel this road alone, without hesitating or
looking back, shall be purified by Fire, by Water, and by Air; and if he
can surmount the fear of death, he shall emerge from the bosom of the
Earth. Then he shall re-enter the Light and claim the right of preparing
himself for the reception of the Mysteries of the Great Goddess Isis."

The trembling Neophyte first met in his journey three disguised men,
armed with swords, who sought to frighten him, first by their appearance
and noise, and then by enumerating the dangers that awaited him in his
journey if he continued.

If his courage did not falter here, he was permitted to pass on to
the Hall of Fire. This hall was lined with burning material, and the floor
was a grate painted flame color. Thru this hall he was obliged to go
quickly to escape the effects of the flames and heat.

He next came to a wide channel fed with water from the Nile, over
which he had to swim with a small lamp in his hand, which afforded all
the light he had.

On reaching the other side, he found a narrow passage leading to a
landing place about six feet square, with movable floor. On each side
were stone walls, and behind metal wheels were fixed. In front was a
door, opening inward, and preventing any farther advance.

In trying to turn two large rings annexed to the door, in hopes of
continuing his journey, the wheels began to revolve, producing a terrific
effect, the floor gave way, leaving him suspended by the arms over apparently a deep abyss, up from which came a violent current of cold air,
which extinguished the lamp, leaving him totally in darkness.

In this process of trial, the Neophyte was exposed to the action of
the Four Elements, fire, air, water, earth.

After the risk of falling into an unknown depth had continued for a
moment, the floor resumed its original position, the wheels stopped, and
the door opened, disclosing the sanctuary of Isis, the High Priestess,
illuminated with a blaze of light, where her priests were assembled, in
two ranks, clad in ceremonial robes, and bearing the mysterious Symbols
of the Order, singing hymns in praise of their divinity. They greeted
and congratulated the Neophyte on his courage and escape from the dangers
which had surrounded him.

The entrance to the sanctuary was constructed in the pedestal of the triple statue of Osiris, Isis and Horus. The walls were decorated with various allegorical figures, symbols of the Egyptian Mysteries as presented in the pictures of Major Arcana, among which were others, but those particularly prominent were:

1. A Serpent casting an egg out of its mouth -- a symbol of all things by the rays of the Sun.

2. A Serpent coiled in the form of a Circle, holding its tail in its mouth -- a symbol of Eternity.

3. The Double Tau, a symbol of the Positive and Negative Forces of the Macrocosm which creates all things.

4. The Sphinx, a symbol of the Four Elements of Creation.

5. The Caduceus, a symbol of the Creative Principle.

This was what may be termed the first degree of initiation in the mysteries of the High Priestess, all the details of which were never known to any but the initiates themselves.

Card 21, The World

This is the companion card of the Priestess, who continues as the actress. She has now changed her costume by removing her robe and appearing with only a blue scarf over her left shoulder, extending down and over the generative center of the body.

The phenomenal World is called Nature. It is the world we see, and cannot come from nothing. Neither was it created in six days by the church God.

The visible world is a picture produced by the condensation of the Four Elements, represented by the Four Beasts of the Egyptian Sphinx, which the Bible says Ezekiel saw in his vision, and presented in a manner to deceive the masses and conceal the facts.

Hotema expressed the opinion in his "Cosmic Creation" that Laplace got the hint of his Nebular Cosmogony from Ezekiel's vision. The postulate was bitterly condemned by the Mother Church because it exploded the creation fable of the first chapter of Genesis. But it was embraced by science as the logical solution of the riddle.

Now comes a nuclear astrophysicist of Canada who asserts that the universe evolved from a vast cloud of hydrogen gas, and the constant reshuffling of the nuclei of the elements finally created all the elements now known on the earth.

The "wheels" mentioned in the Ezekiel (1:15) simply represent the Zodiakos, the symbolism of which applies to the World and to every kind of cosmic force and element of the universe.

The elliptic garland in Card 21 contains 22 groups of three leaves, eleven groups on each side. The top and bottom of the garland have a horizontal eight-shaped-binding, similar to the Life Link over the head of the Magician in card 1, and over the head of the woman in card 8, which is to indicate the macrocosmic character of the wreath, and the ancient axion, "As above, so below."

There is no change in structure of the garland from top to bottom, which is to indicate that the physical world is composed of the same elements as the astral world, the only difference being that in the physical world they are visible because they are condensed.

The dancing girl in the center of the wreath holds in each hand a spiralistic wand, the spirals in the right hand turning clockwise, and those in the left turning counter-clockwise, symbolizing Involution and Evolution.

C. C. Zain said: "As in truth the Sun is the source of all physical, mental and emotional power expressed on earth, the planets merely refracting its various attributes, and the signs acting as sounding-boards for such expression, so Arcanum 21, signifying perfection, union and attainment on all three planes, corresponds to the Sun." -- The Tarot, p. 406.

The High Priestess and the World Mother are one. They are symbolized in the Bible as the Woman clothed with the Sun, the moon under her feet, and upon her head a crown of twelve stars. -- Rev. 12:1.

Not a preacher in Christendom possesses the fundamental knowledge of Creation to make him competent to interpret this symbolism of the Ancient Astrologers, condemned by the church as "superstitious heathens."

The Sun signifies the fecundating agent, the moon implies generation, and the crown of twelve stars indicates the twelve signs of the Zodiakos.

As the sunshine striking the earth causes the earth to produce, so the Sun shines on Woman, symbolizing the World Mother, and she produces.

Ancient symbolism was an esoteric process of illustrating cosmic principles and elements in action. In had no reference whatever to the imaginary work of an imaginary god and a crucified savior, as taught by the church.

Polarity is prominently presented by the two pillars, one white and one black, between which the Priestess sits. Polarity is the Creative Principle. In the case of living creatures it is called Sexuality.

Nothing can manifest objectively without the dualistic properties of Polarity. That is the only god of Creation.

Without Polarity there would be no Universe and no Creation. And this Creative Principle is not the property nor power of the church God, but that of the Conscious, Intelligent, Infinite, Omnipotent Atom.

It was around this Creative Principle that revolved all the mythology, symbology and secrecy of the ancient philosophies and religions. Excerpted from Cosmic Creation by Hotema.

THE EMPRESS.

JUDGEMENT.

Chapter IX

CARD 3, THE EMPRESS & CARD 20, RESURRECTION

Card 3, The Empress

This card presents a woman, with two great wings, which are absent in some pictures, seated upon the Throne of the Sun, and seen full face.

In her right hand is an escutcheon bearing an Eagle with outspread wings, and in her left she holds a Scepter surmounted by a globe and the symbol of Venus. She is adorned with a crown of twelve stars, and has a lunar crescent under her feet. In front of her, in some pictures, a field of grain is maturing.

The Empress appears in the Bible, mentioned as follows:

"And there appeared a great wonder in heaven; a woman clothed with the sun, and the moon under her feet, and upon her head a crown of twelve stars" (Rev. 12:1).

The Empress represents all phases of the phenomenal world. She represents growth, unfoldment, product. She signifies the results of the active principles reflected in Cards 1 and 2.

Being "clothed with the sun" implies universal fecundity. The Eagle (Scorpio) signifies sexuality. The moon under her feet indicates generation. The Scepter, crowned by the symbol of Venus, represents the sacred office of Motherhood.

-64-

Her diadem, with 12 stars, indicates that the Empress personifies the laws and powers of the Macrocosm which rule the Microcosm, as symbolized in the twelve signs of the Zodiakos.

The total, combined qualities of the Empress signify the Cycle of Life. She represents the gate of entrance into the phenomenal world, as into the Garden of Venus.

To complete the Cycle, she holds the secret of the path that extends out into the vast realm of darkness of the unknown, -- which is the theme of the next card, 20, Resurrection (Reincarnation). (Or, in some cards, Judgement).

One of the purposes of initiation in the Ancient Mysteries was to teach the "man of darkness," who had been prepared, tested, and accepted, and who is symbolized in the Bible as a Lamb facing "sacrifice" (Rev. 5:6), that golden secret of the mysterious Astral World, lying just over the hill which all living things must travel, and which secret the church has tried so hard to hide from the masses.

If the true and correct knowledge of that secret were taught to the masses, it would ruin Christianity. That is the reason why the ancient libraries and ancient scrolls were destroyed after the birth of Christianity.

Card 20, Resurrection (Reincarnation)

We shall now show where the biblical makers got their account of the Resurrection which they craftily wove around their fabulous Jesus.

A million years ago the Doctrine of the Resurrection and Reincarnation developed from the observation of the cyclical processes of Creation.

The Masters of Lemuria saw man as a part of nature, not apart from nature.

That man is in some way akin to nature, not even the most positive evolutionist will attempt to deny.

The Lemurian Masters realized that the link which binds man to all nature is something far more than akinness. They saw in man something far greater than flowers of the field.

Man is the crowning glory of all Creation. He is the god of all the earth, -- a fact recognized even by the biblical makers (Gen. 1:26).

For ages throughout the ancient world, the Resurrection of the god Sol, under different names in different ages and among different nations, was celebrated on March 25 with elaborate ceremonies of great rejoicing.

With the Resurrection of the Sun from the southern hemisphere, came the Resurrection of the grass and flowers, with dormant forests turning green with new foliage.

All nature rose from the dead.

This cosmic event illustrates the Law of Cyclic Manifestation, the basic law which teaches the inspiring lessons that death is not what it seems.

For out of death there cometh the Resurrection, the Reincarnation of Life.

From the death of winter there comes in the spring the Resurrection of all the vegetation of the earth. Is man less than the flowers?

These facts of ages of observation taught the Masters that as the Law of Cyclic Manifestation rules the vegetable kingdom, it must also rule the animal kingdom. For the Law is one, and Life is one, and there could not be one law for the life of the vegetable kingdom and another for the life of the animal kingdom.

If flowers die and return to a future life, so does man.

The manifestation of the Creative Life is cyclic in all kingdoms, and applies to animal life as fully as to vegetal life.

So, upon this solid foundation the Ancient Masters built their Doctrine of the Resurrection and Reincarnation.

The biblical makers were exceedingly careful to keep out of the Bible all direct reference to Reincarnation. To hide the facts and deceive the masses, they changed the word Reincarnation to "regeneration" (Matt. 19:28); Titus 3:5).

Then they applied the Cyclic Law of Life only to their Jesus.

Ouspensky wrote:

"And I saw an icy plain. A chain of snow-covered mountains shut off the horizon. A cloud rose and grew until it covered a quarter of the sky.

"In the midst of the cloud there appeared two fiery wings. And, behold, I saw the messenger of the Empress.

"I saw him raise his trumpet, and he blew a loud blast. And the plain trembled, and with loud reverberating echoes the mountains answered.

"And one after another of the graves in the plain began to open, and out of them came forth people -- young children and old men and women. And they stretched out their arms to the messenger of the Empress, and tried to catch the sound of the trumpet.

"In that sound of the trumpet I felt the smile of the Empress. And in the opening graves I saw unfolding flowers and smelt their fragrance.

"And now I understood the mystery of Birth and Death." == New Model of Universe.

Ye must be born again says the Bible (Jn. 3:3, 5, 7).

The clearest account of the ancient Doctrine of Resurrection (Reincarnation) in the Bible, appears in the epistles of Paul.

Paul explained, in his terminology as recorded in the Bible, that death is the process of releasing the Ego from the body; that death is simply a CHANGE OF STATE, not the ANNIHILATION OF BEING.

He called it a "mystery", and attempted to explain the "mystery" by describing the dual nature of man, calling them celestial and terrestrial bodies, and declaring that DEATH is simply separation of the two. According to the Bible, he said:

"There are celestial bodies and bodies terrestrial. But the glory (nature) of the celestial is one (thing), and the glory of the terrestrial is another. ...

"Behold, I show you a mystery: We shall not sleep (in death), but we shall be changed; in a moment, in the twinkling of an eye, at the last trumpet."

"For the trumpet (of Gabriel) shall sound, and the dead shall be raised incorruptible, and we shall be changed (from mortality to immortality).

"For this corruptible (body) must put on incorruption, and this mortal (body) must put on immortality. (The celestial body, Ego, separates from, or leaves the terrestrial body).

"So when this corruptible shall have put on incorruption, and this mortal shall have put on immortality, then shall be brought to pass the saying that is written:

"Death is swallowed up in victory (Is. 28:8). O death, where is thy sting? O grave, where is thy victory." (1 Cor. 15:40-55).

We know not what Paul's exact statements were. It is certain the biblical makers rendered the phraseology as ambiguous as they could, to hide the facts and make it more difficult to be understood by the man of darkness.

And to increase the ambiguity, the biblical makers fraudulently added verses 56-58 to Chapter 15, in order to mislead the masses and to weave in their gospel Jesus, who was utterly unknown to Paul.

An 8th grade pupil can detect the abrupt break in context between verses 55 and 56.

We must observe in particular that Paul said, "The trumpet shall sound, and the dead shall be raised incorruptible."

Not just those who believe in the gospel Jesus. But all the dead shall be raised incorruptible. There is no limit; there are no qualifications.

This scene created by Paul's statements is clearly presented in Card 20, titled "Judgement", or the "Last Judgement." According to the Bible, the title should be Resurrection or Reincarnation.

There is still another feature presented in the picture that appears in the Bible.

In the picture there are seven lines radiating from the bell of the trumpet blown by the angel, indicating seven basic tones. This takes us directly to Chapter 10 of the last book of the Bible, as follows:

"And I saw another mighty angel come down from heaven, clothed with a cloud; and a rainbow was upon his head, and his face was luminous like the sun, and his feet like pillars of fire.

"And he had in his hand a little scroll unrolled. He set his right foot upon the sea, and his left foot on the earth, and cried with a loud voice; and seven thunders uttered their voices.

"When the seven thunders had uttered their voices, I was about to write (down the teachings); but I heard a voice from the sky saying to me:

" 'Seal up (the teachings) which the seven thunders uttered, and write them not' " (Rev. 10:1-4).

Those voices of the seven thunders appear to relate directly to the seven basic tones of the trumpet of the angel in Card 20.

And furthermore, it is clear that the voices of the seven thunders were esoteric secrets not intended for the exoteric and the profane; for they were not to be recorded.

What were the teachings of the voices of the seven thunders?

The angel appearing here, clothed with a cloud, and a rainbow upon his head, similates the angel in Card 20, who blows the seven basic tones, and "the dead are rising from their tombs"; and "all figures", said Dr. Waite, "are as one in the wonder, adoration and ecstacy expressed by their attitude."

The trumpeter is termed the angel Gabriel, representing the element of water, as indicated by his blue robe.

- - - - - - - - - - -

The correct interpretation of the symbolism of Cards 3 and 20 shows the source of some of the ancient symbology and allegory contained in the New Testament.

These crafty biblical makers not only had possession of the 22 missing Trumps Major, but understood the interpretation thereof, and interpolated in various parts of the New Testament some of that interpretation.

The biblical makers state that their Jesus cried out with a loud voice (the voice of the seven thunders), (and) yielded up the ghost, ... "and the graves were opened, and many bodies of the saints which slept arose" (Mat. 27:50, 52).

We are dealing with the Cycle of Life, and shall notice it again in considering Card 10, the Wheel of Life, and Card 13, the Wheel of Death.

Cards 3, 10, 13, and 20 should be studied together.

Doctrine of Resurrection

The doctrine of a resurrection to a future and eternal life existed among almost all ancient nations from the earliest times.

The Egyptians, in their mysteries, taught a final resurrection of the Ego.

The Jews adopted the doctrine after the seventy years of captivity, borrowing it from the Babylonians. They had no literature of their own until after the captivity, being just a group of sheep herders, unlearned and ignorant. They returned from Babylonia educated people and then began to produce their literature, copying what they had learned from the Babylonians.

The Brahmans and Buddhists, the Etruscans, Greeks, Romans, Druids and Scandinavians, taught the doctrine of a resurrection of the Ego to a future and eternal life.

That event in man's existence called Death, which marks the transition from the material and visible to the invisible, astral world, was not regarded in ancient times as it is now in the Christian world.

In point of fact, there is no such condition as death, extinction, annihilation. There is no ending and no beginning. It is an axiom of science that something cannot come from nothing. And the something which comes, must, under the law of Like begets Like, present in character, if not indegree, the qualities of the producer.

And so, as Life in the visible world comes from pre-existent Life in the invisible world, the Life which comes has no beginning and no ending. Hotema says in his "Pre-Existence of Man": --

"As the Macrocosm produces the Microcosm, under the law that Like begets Like, the Microcosm must illustrate and describe with perfect precision, the characteristics,qualities and properties of the Macrocosm."

Material forms change, but the Entities which inhabit the forms change

The substance of which man's body is composed is as eternal as the Ego which dwells in that body, as Hotema has explained in "Cosmic Creation."

THE EMPEROR.

THE SUN.

Chapter X

CARD 4, THE EMPEROR & CARD 19, THE SUN

Half Truths

Since the Tarot first appeared in Europe early in the 14th century, many able authors have attempted to interpret its pictorial symbolism, including such learned men as Eliphas Levi, Dr. Arthur E. Waite, and the greatest occultists in this country.

A complete and correct interpretation of this symbolism is impossible for him who does not understand the esoteric message of the ancient philosophy, and who is not competent to fill in all the details of the ancient maxim, "As above, so below."

What was the basic philosophy contained in the Ancient Scrolls from which the Bible was compiled?

That is what we are going to consider and explain in our interpretation of the cartomancy of the Tarot. We shall expose the crafty manner in which the scheming priesthood compiled the "Word of God" from the Ancient Scrolls, and freely employed the trick of using half truths to deceive the masses.

These men not only had possession of the Tarot, but understood the inner meaning of its symbolism.

-70-

For instance, they say in the picture of Card 20 how the "dead" rose up from their graves at the sound of the trumpet of the "strong angel" Gabriel, and mentioned it in the Bible (1 Cor. 15:52).

The various commentators have called this card "The Last Judgement," and Dr. Waite wrote:

"An angel sounds his trumpet 'per sepulchra regionum,' and the dead arise. ... It should be noted (in the picture) that all the (rising) figures are as one in the wonder, adoration and ecstacy expressed by their attitudes."

It is perfectly obvious that the correct title of this card is The Resurrection. And yet that title does not exactly express the true meaning. But the biblical makers took that title, applied it to their Jesus, and then deliberately and definitely excluded from that category all the rest of mankind, contrary to the ancient philosophy.

Here is another instance of the employment of a half truth to deceive the masses. We shall consider more of these half truths and show how deceptive and dangerous they are.

Image and Likeness of God

The Bible states that God made man in His image and likeness (Gen. 1:26, 27).

That statement is a "half truth". Man is definitely and completely made in the image and likeness of "God". The big trick or catch lies in the true meaning of the word "God".

Here is an example of a "half truth". The mystery of both "God" and man vanishes when the "half truth" is replaced by the whole truth.

What is Man? Who has the answer? The answer will explain everything.

We shall discover this church "God" by discovering the nature of Life and the Constitution of Man.

For some reason, the science of living creatures in general, and of man in particular, has not made much progress. There must be a definite cause for this lack of knowledge in the field of Anthropology and Biology.

This lack of progress may be due to fear of what the findings will reveal. To the fact that discoveries might result which will destroy the profitable systems that live on ignorance and thrive on darkness. Hence, there may be "method in this madness", and "science in this ignorance".

Man is an indivisible whole of a mysterious complexity. He is classed as an animal, but such classification fails to fit him. There is a great, unbridgeable gulf between the lowest man and the highest animal. The evolutionists have been unable to bridge this gulf after a century of labor.

That great doctor, Alexis Carrel, visualized man as a god. He said: "Man stands above all things." The Bible agrees. It says that man has dominion over every living thing on earth. (Gen. 1:28).

But the teachings of the scheming priesthood present a different picture. Of all the living things on earth, man alone is the only one whose future is dark and dismal. He is a cringing slave who must cower and quail in abject fear before a God that will show him no mercy, save on one condition -- that he believe in and worship the Son of God, the gospel Jesus.

We can know little about Man as long as we neglect to study Mind, Consciousness, Intelligence and Vitality. These four inexplicable qualities constitute Man, and science admits that as to these it knows almost nothing.

The late Dr. Robert A. Millikan, world renowned scientist, head of the California Institute of Technology, authority on Cosmic Rays, said:

"I cannot explain why I am alive rather than dead. The physiologists can tell me much about the mechanical and chemical processes of my body, but they cannot say why I am alive" (Collier's, Oct. 24, 1925).

Yes, and much that is taught by the physiologists about the mechanical and chemical processes of the body is pure hogwash and hokum. The great Carrel condemned it in these words:

"The childish physico-chemical conceptions of human beings, in which so many physiologists and physicians still believe, have to be definitely abandoned" (Man The Unknown, p. 108).

Why abandoned? Because they are erroneous, false, misleading.

No clear, simple, reasonable representation of Man has ever been presented in modern times. No method has so far been developed that is capable of apprehending Man simultaneously in his entirety, his parts, and his relation to the Universe. Or to God if you prefer.

Man will continue to remain a mystery to himself until science discovers his relationship to the world to which he belongs, and of which he is not only a part, but the highest part on earth, of the world in which he lives, and moves, and has his being (Acts 17:28).

To discover the true nature of Life and the constitution of Man requires knowledge as to the Creative Principle and the Creative Elements.

We must begin with a self-existent Universal Principle, and, by logical reasoning and consistent process, bring that Principle down from the universal to the individual, leaving no gaps to be bridged and no gulfs to be crossed.

In other words, we must reach out and bring down the Macrocosm to the Microcosm, and scientifically affirm of the latter all the distinctive qualities of the former.

The Ancient Masters did that, and they solved the mystery of Man. The Key to the secret is concealed in their maxim, "As above, so below."

To be more explicit, as the Maker, so the Made. For Man must be the image and likeness of his Maker.

That is a fact so obvious and self-evident as to be unrecognized by only those who have no desire to see it. It is the last fact on earth that the church wants Man to discover. For that discovery would ruin the greatest scheme of profit and power the world has ever known.

The scheming men who compiled the Bible, included the substance of the Key of the Masters when they wrote:

· "God created man in his own image, after his own likeness."

These biblical makers knew what the Masters taught. They had the knowledge before them in the ancient scrolls. But they destroyed the precious scrolls to hide that teaching from the eyes of the world.

The orthodox Christians are in for a terrific shock when we compare the biblical statement with the substance of the scrolls, and, by the use of that evidence, reveal the true nature of that God who made man in his image and likeness.

To all appearances, the biblical statements seem to be in perfect harmony with the ancient maxim, "As above, so below".

It is to a certain extent. But at this particular point there is involved a deep, dark plot, and that plot has been well concealed. The time has come when it shall be revealed.

Just exactly what did the ancient scrolls say? Where are they now? Why were ancient libraries burned and ancient writings destroyed after the Bible was made? Why did Archbishop Chrysostom, in the middle of the 5th century, feel so happy when he boasted that --

"Every trace of the old philosophy and literature of the ancient world has vanished from the face of the earth" (Bible Myths, Doane, p. 436).

Why did the invention of the printing press in the 15th century so badly frighten the church that Cardinal Wolsey, Bishop of London, in a convocation of his clergy, said:

"If we do not destroy this dangerous invention, it will one day destroy us" (Doane, p. 438)?

Nothing frightens the church so greatly as the spread of knowledge.

By their own acts and deeds the church authorities have presented the evidence which convicts them of the crimes they have committed and concealed.

When the chief custodian of the great Alexandrian library was secretly warned of the plot to burn the library, he hastily collected some of the most precious scrolls and shipped them off to Arabia for safety.

When this was discovered by the church authorities, they were shocked and instituted the Crusades in an attempt to recover these scrolls and destroy them.

The Crusades lasted close to two centuries (1095-1291). Another pious lie was told of their purpose. It was to recover the "Holy Land" from the heathens.

The scrolls were never recovered by the church.

The church could not make the masses believe the earth was flat when the Masters had taught that it is round. That knowledge was taught by the Chaldeans and Egyptians for thousands of years before the world ever heard of Christianity.

The church could not make the masses believe in its anthropomorphic God, when the Masters had taught for millions of years that the glorious Sun is the Father Of Light and the Giver Of Life.

That knowledge was contained in the Ancient Scrolls, and still appears in the Bible. It definitely states that *God is a Consuming Fire* (Heb. 12:29).

We are now coming close to the great secret, "As above, so below", follow us closely and keep all these points in mind.

Origin of the Bible

The origin of the Christian Bible is cloaked in mystery. None of the original scrolls of the Old Testament are extant.

The oldest Jewish religious documents do not predate the 8th century A.D., and the oldest manuscripts of the Old Testament now extant is dated 916 A.D. Quite young.

Before the 14th century there was no English Bible. It began to take shape under John Wycliff and his co-workers. They collected material here and there, and completed their translation of it into an English version in 1384 A.D.

Then other versions came so fast and were so discordant and corrupted, that in 1408 the English enacted a law prohibiting the translation of Latin Bibles into English.

Tyndale's Bible, prepared by him after he was driven from England for translating the Bible into English, was the most loved, the most hated, and the most successful of all.

One half of the Christians bought Tyndale's Bible to read, and the other half to burn.

Most Christians would be amazed if they read more about the making of their Bible and less about the hogwash and hokum contained in the Bible.

For the Bible is the last place to look for a truthful, factual description of God and of Man.

When we shall have found that description, then there will come to be understood the secret meaning of the statement, God created man in his own image, after his own likeness.

The true nature of Life and the constitution of Man were contained in the ancient Scrolls.

That knowledge, if presented now, would clarify the modern confusion surrounding Life and Man. It had to be concealed and destroyed so the Mother Church could grow rich and powerful by selling the misled masses its God and its Jesus.

Now has come the time when an unprejudiced attempt shall be made to give the masses, in simple terms, the true nature of God and a correct description of Man.

Lucky is he who reads this work and has the intelligence to understand what he reads.

And no one shall seal the sayings contained herein: For the time is at hand (Rev. 22:10).

The Sphinx

Had the Wisdom of the Ancient Masters not been well recorded in stone and preserved in mysterious symbols and hieroglyphs, the Christian world would today have none of it.

As we search the encyclopedias for an interpretation of these ancient symbols, we are purposely led further astray by the crafty work of the church.

The public is not aware of the fact that the encyclopedias are censored by the church as to all things touching upon gods, religions and ancient symbols. For no concern would think of publishing anything relating to these subjects without first consulting the church authorities.

Hence, to the masses, the ancient Sphinx is just another silly image that came from the hands of the ancient heathens. The layman is certain it represents nothing more than ancient superstition. That's exactly the way the church wants him to feel about it.

But that layman is going to be surprised when he reads our interpretation of this ancient image.

Of all the ancient symbols that have come down to us, the Sphinx is one of the oldest and greatest.

This strange image, which means nothing to the layman, is found in all countries of the ancient world. It went down in the sea with continents that have sunk and vanished and disappeared. It is found in the ruins of cities built at sea-level millions of years ago, before there was a single mountain on the face of the earth.

The ruins of some of these cities are now on mountain tops three miles high. Read the story in Cosmic Creation by Hotema.

Sphinx is the Greek name of this image, and means to bind or draw tight, to squeeze. The Egyptians called the Sphinx Hu, or Neb.

Encyclopedias say the Sphinx probably originated in Egypt, and was borrowed from there by Greek art. They further say that in the mythology of ancient Egypt, the Sphinx represented the solar deity, Ra, and adds:

"All nations of antiquity seem to have held those monstrous beings in various shapes and forms as objects of awe, compelling adoration and worship."

Yes, very true -- but why?

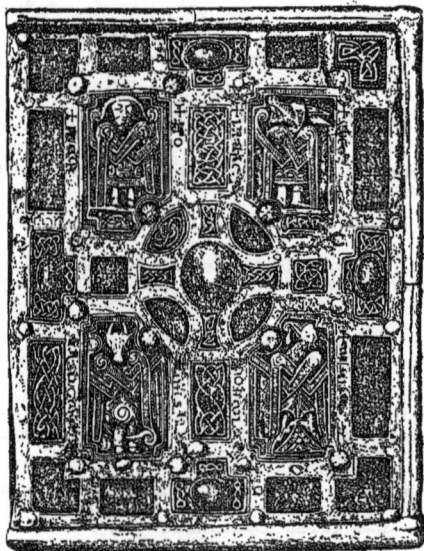

There is a secret reason, and that secret we are going to unfold.

That ancient secret was known to the early church fathers. To hide the secret, they destroyed the ancient scrolls. Then they feigned ignorance when they prepared the literature in which they gave us their fraudulant version of the history of the ancient world and the ancient symbols. That false version is what we have in our histories and encyclopedias.

No sensible interpretation of the Sphinx appears in the encyclopedias, nor in the Bible, and yet that symbol was hoary with age and its symbolism was well known when the various books of the Bible were written.

Many wild, sensational and unintelligible references to the Sphinx appear in the Bible. But the description is such that the layman would never suspect it referred to the Sphinx.

Ezekiel saw a whirlwind come out of the north, a great cloud, and a fire infolding itself ... and out of the midst thereof came the likeness of four living creatures.

Then there follows a wild description of the Sphinx, mixed up with the Zodiakos, the description of which is just as sensational as that of the Sphinx. (Chap. 1:4, 5, 15-21).

We have a big surprise for the layman when we interpret this symbology in Ezekiel. It may appear sensational and unintelligible to him and the preacher, yet it conceals and covers cosmic facts that reveal the nature of Life and the constitution of Man.

Daniel saw strange sights in a vision. These visions were very convenient for those old boys to hide behind.

What did Daniel see in his vision? The four winds of heaven striving upon the great sea, and four great beasts came up from the sea. Then there follows a sensational description of the Sphinx (7:1-7).

In Revelation the same four beasts appear in the midst of the throne. The first was like a lion (Leo), the second like a calf (Taurus), the third had a man's face (Aquarius), and the fourth was like a flying eagle (Scorpio) (4:6, 7).

THE FOUR ELEMENTS

We are cutting closely to an ancient secret. Here are the Four Fixed Signs of the Zodiakos which form the Cross of Life.

Why does the Sphinx, constituted of the same quartette, appear so often in the Bible and play such an important part?

There is a highly important and surprising reason, and it does not represent ancient stupidity and superstition. The reader should keep that in mind as we proceed.

Now, the deluded theologian says that only God can grow a tree. And the unthinking, mind-controlled multitude believes.

But what does he mean by God? That same old question keeps coming up, and no one has a reasonable or sensible answer.

The observation and experience of millions of years show that --

1. Solar Heat   3. Water
2. Air   4. Soil

-77-

produce not only trees and the vegetal kingdom, but the animal kingdom also.

: Without these Four Elements, all the gods invented by man would be useless and helpless, and there could be made nothing that is or has been made.

And with these Four Elements, there is no place and no need for gods.

We are now uncovering a highly important, very ancient secret, which the church buried so deeply in the 4th century, that its discovery and resurrection appeared truly impossible.

In the 19th century there lived a great French Mystic by the name of Alphonse Louis Constant. He did much writing under the pseudonym of Eliphas Levi. In his History of Magic (1853) he described the lost and hidden message of the Ancient Masters which is concealed in the Sphinx. This is what he said:

"The symbolical tetrad, represented in the Ancient Mysteries by the four forms of the Sphinx -- man, eagle, lion and bull - corresponded with the Four Principle Elements of the universe — earth, water, air and fire.

"These four zodiac signs, with all their analogies, explained the one sacred WORD hidden in all the sanctuaries of the ancient world ... Moreover, the sacred WORD was never pronounced; it was always spelt, and expressed in four words, which are the sacred words Yod-He-Vau-He."

J H V H

Now we are moving in on one of the ancient secrets which the church has tried so hard to hide.

According to the Old Testament, God had the occasion to give himself a new name. In speaking to Moses, as one man to another, he said:

"I appeared unto Abraham, unto Isaac, and unto Jacob, by the name of God Almighty, but by the name J H V H (written Je-Ho-Vah in the Bible) was I not known to them" (Exodus 6:3).

And so, this God not only appeared unto Moses, but here states that he appeared also unto others. But the Bible says that no man hath seen God at any time (Jn. 1:18).

What does the Bible contain that one can believe?

This Hebrew word consisted of four letters J H V H, pronounced Yod-He-Vau-He, but it was strictly forbidden to the Jews to pronounce it, and was called the Ineffable Name.

All this prohibiting and forbidding was for the purpose of keeping the masses in darkness, under the control of the priesthood, and to conceal the fact that the Ineffable Name applied not to a God, but to the Four Elements of Creation, symbolized by the Sphinx.

The Four Letters, J H V H, concealed a deep symbolical secret.

The first letter, called Yod, expressed the active principle(initiative).

The second, He, the passive principle (receptive). The third, Vau, equilibrium, form also a link or bridge that united the two, the active and passive principles. This union produced the next step in creation, the second He, regarded as the offspring of the first two.

Here is the Eternal Trinity. All mythology of the ancient religions revolved round this Trinitarian Center. The Christians changed it to the Father, Son, and the Holy Ghost.

A study of the Sacred Name which represented the Four Elements, and the finding of one or more of the elements in everything, constituted the chief goal of Kaballistic philosophy.

So, the Kaballists held that these Four Elements permeate and compose everything in the universe, and that is what the church says of its God, in these words:

"By a paradox that defies the reasoning faculty, but which is readily resolved intuitively, God is apart from, and independent of the universe, and yet he permeates every atom of it."

By discovering these Four Elements in objects and phenomena of quite different categories, between which the man in darkness sees nothing in common, the Initiate of the Ancient Mysteries sees the analogy between all objects and all phenomena, and is thus convinced that all things are constructed and constituted of the same elements, according to the same law.

The concept is quite clear: If the Ineffable Name (Four Elements) is in everything, then everything is analogous to the whole, -- the atom analogous to the universe, man analogous to the sun, and all analogous to the Ineffable Name, J H V H.

So, the Ancient Masters said, "As above, so below." And the church improved it by stating that God created man in his image and likeness.

It was to suppress and destroy this ancient secret that the church authorities had the ancient literature destroyed and the ancient libraries burned.

The secret meaning of the Sacred Word, J H V H, had to be destroyed in order to make safe the way of the anthropomorphic God of the church.

Card 4, The Emperor

"He pronounced Daleth, and referred it to Fertility. He crowned it, combined and formed with the Sun in the Universe, the third day of the week, and the right nostril of man." — Sepher Yetzirah, 22.

The 4th letter of the Hebrew alphabet is Daleth (D), the 3rd of the seven double letters. It is combined with the Sun and referred to fertility.

The Sun has a dual aspect in that while (1) in its positive aspect it is the fructifying power which stimulates fertility, (2) in its negative aspect it scorches, kills, produces putrefaction, and causes the opposite of fertility, or sterility.

In Card 4 we see man seated upon a cubic stone, on one side of which is carved an eagle with outstretched wings.

The eagle is the power of sexuality uplifted, or Scorpio transformed.

On the other side of the stone is carved the head of a Ram, the first sign of the Zodiakos, Aries, a fiery, cardinal sign, in which the Sun is exalted, or raised to its highest level of power. The color corresponding to Aries is scarlet. The musical tone is C-natural.

The orange background in the upper part of the picture refers to the exaltation of the Sun in Aries. Below it are red mountains, of igneous rock.

The scepter in the Emperor's right hand is a modified Venus symbol, golden in color, being another reference to the exaltation of the Sun in Aries.

This scepter is also one form of the Egyptian ankh, or symbol of Life.

The Emperor is the consort of the Empress, Card 3. He is, in fact, essentially identical with the Magician, Card 1, after the latter's union with the High Priestess, Card 2, has transformed her into the Empress, and made him the progenitor of her children.

Ouspensky wrote: --

I saw the Emperor on a high throne of stone, decorated with an eagle and the head of a ram.

A golden helmet gleamed on his brow. His long white beard fell over his purple mantle. In one hand he held a sphere, symbol of the earth or his possessions, and in the other a scepter in the form of the Egyptian cross, the symbol of his power over creation.

"I am the Great Law", said the Emperor.

"I am the Ineffable Name, J H V H.

"The four letters of the Name are in me, and I am in everything.

"I am in the four principles; I am in the four elements; I am in the four quarters of the earth.

"I am in the four signs of the Tarot.

"I am action; I am resistance; I am completion; I am result.

"For him who knows the way to see me, there are no mysteries on the earth.

"As the earth contains fire, air and water, and as the fourth letter of the Ineffable Name contains the first three and itself becomes the first, so my scepter contains the complete Triangle and bears in itself the seed of a new Triangle."

While the Emperor was speaking, his helmet and the golden armour visible beneath his mantle shone ever more brightly, until I could no longer bear the radiance and dropped my eyes.

"And when I tried to raise my eyes again, before me was an all-pervading radiance, and light and fire. And I fell prostrate worshipping the Fiery Word, the Living Fire."

We have quoted from Ouspensky the words of the actor who played the part of the Emperor in the Ancient Drama. Now we shall quote the words of the biblical compilers, which they put in the mouth of their talking God:

"Let us make man in our image, after our own likeness; and let them have dominion over the fish of the sea, the fowls of the air, over the cattle, and over all the earth, and every creeping thing upon the earth" (Gen. 1:26).

Observe how craftily the scheming church fathers paraphrased the language of the actor in the ancient drama, in which the Neophyte was taught the nature of Life and the constitution of his own body.

Also, we must notice the fraudulent process of evolution appearing in the John gospel by which the Sacred WORD was metamorphosed into the church God:

The Word was in the beginning; and
The Word was with God; and
The Word was God (Jn. 1:1).

Now we know what the Word means and what God means. The sly biblical editors took the Sacred WORD, which symbolized the Four Elements, and transformed it into their living, breathing God.

This is an excellent illustration of a half truth. God represents the Four Elements as we have shown, and as such representative, is in everything in the Universe. But so different from the God described by the preacher.

How are the misled masses to know that? Who will tell them? And how many of the blind believers in the church God can be convinced when told?

We must not overlook the other half truth. Man is created in the image and likeness of God.

Of what is God created? The Four Elements. Of what is Man created? The Four Elements. So lies become truth and truth becomes a lie.

Card 19, The Sun

"In the beginning," says a Sanscrit hymn, "arose the Source of Golden Light. He was the only born Lord of all that is. He gives light, he gives life, and he gives strength."

Certain scientists declare that the Sun is a gigantic generator, and every= thing existing on the earth consists of solar electricity in countless forms.

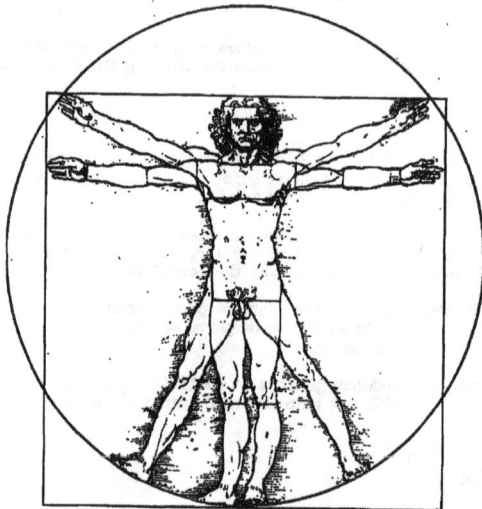

All the motions, visible and invisible, that transpire in the mineral, vegetal, animal and humanal kingdoms, and in their multifarious operations are produced by solar electricity, called Astral Light by the Ancient Masters, the universal agent that maintains the harmony and order of the universe.

The ancient sun-myth was the core of all religion and philosophy on earth among intelligent people before the birth of the Roman Catholic Church in the 4th century.

That exalted intelligence of Ageless Wisdom, on the mount illuminated by Solar Radiance, was destroyed when Christianity submerged the Sun Glory of the ancient world in the body of a man, transforming the Sun God into the Son of God, and making it necessary to invent a God as the father of that fabulous Son.

In converting the Solar God of the Universe into an actual man of Christianity, the Roman Empire passed forthwith out of the Light of Learning into the dreadful shadows of the Dark Ages.

And never forget that that period of intellectual darkness cannot end until the Bright Glow of Solar Wisdom has been resurrected and enthroned to enlighten benighted modernity.

The discoveries of modern scientists fully confirm the Fire Philosophy of the Ancient Masters.

The New York Times of Nov. 25, 1932, reported the announcement of Dr. George W. Crile, noted scientist of the Cleveland Laboratories, that he had discovered in the center of every cell of protoplasm, tiny foci of energy which he termed "hot points" or "radiogens", with estimated temperatures from 3,000 to 6,000 degrees of heat.

Crile found that protoplasm emitted radiations of various wave lengths, "some as powerful as those emitted by the sun," he said, and added:

"The sun shines in the protoplasm of animals and plants, therefore they can confer such chemical affinities on atoms as are conferred by the sun itself."

Who would think there are "hot points" in man and animals on the order of the temperature of the surface of the sun?

If we could look into protoplasm with an eye capable of infinite magnification, we might expect to see the radiogens, spaced like stars, as suns in infinite miniature.

Without exaggeration, the concept may be taken to mean, that within the very flesh of man there burns the fierce fire of the sun, and within man's body glows infinitely small counterparts of the stars.

These findings by Crile but confirm the statements of the Ancient Masters, that the atoms in man's body are the same as those of the suns and stars. "As above, so below," they said.

This report by Crile, which fell more or less unheeded on the prejudiced ears of the scientists, at last records the discovery of the direct point of contact between man and his universe.

This discovery by Crile, after sixteen hundred years of obscuration, points the fundamental authenticity of the ancient solar myth, out of which rose all the ancient religion and philosophy.

Scientific discovery has now restored to religion the basic principle, of which it has been bereft for nearly two millennia of darkness.

Religion now returns to its place in the sun, because the sun returns to its place in religion.

So, we see the truth in the statement that "Christ", the essence of Solar Energy, "is all, and in all" (Col. 3:11).

In an old book on the Rosicrucians, published in 1872, the following sentence has stood in the silence of scientific scorn all these years:

"Man has a little spark of the sun in his bosom.... A spark of the original light remains deep down in the interior of every atom" (Rosicrucians, Their Rites and Mysteries, Jennings, p. 211).

A spark of the sun occupies the center of every atom of the body. This radiant gleam of mental light by which mankind may again see to read aright the sacred scrolls of Ancient Wisdom.

Science now finds itself on bended knee before this tiny glint of Solar Light in the heart of every atom. Its mighty force appears when it is released from its prison.

The Sun was the center of the Ageless Wisdom because it is the center of all Life.

This Wisdom was organically constructed about the nucleus of the profound teaching directly related to the phenomena of Life. It was no detached scheme of emotionalism, but an alignment of devotion related to knowledge of the element and fact of Life itself.

The central fact was the presence of a Solar Fragment, a Spark of the Sun, in the body of Man. We call it Ego.

The immortal Ego is a beam of the central sun. This speck of Cosmic Intelligence was the seventh emanation crowning the elementary six, and summing their powers all in itself.

Man, in whom this spark was made local in nature, was the crown and summation of all precedent expression.

All the lower kingdoms are in man, the three sub-mineral, the mineral, vegetal, animal and humanal thus far evolved. They are comprehended in him in the constituency of his four lower vehicles, which make him the composite he is.

By his body and his senses man is linked with the earth. By his consciousness; mind and intelligence of the Ego, he is linked with the stars of the sky, the Astral World.

Head in heaven, body on earth, said the Egyptian Masters: "I am a child of earth and the starry skies." And the church calls them pagans and heathens.

The body is mortal, doomed to temporal extinction. The Ego is an immortal entity, facing a future of eternal existence.

The Egyptian Masters taught that the history of each fragment of Solar Light impounded in a corral of flesh on earth, is a reflected miniature of that of the great Solar Orb itself.

The growth and progress of the tiny spark that is individualized in man, was studied by the masters in the light of its parental analogue in the sky.

So, the basis of the Ageless Wisdom was the course of the Sun thru the Solar year, which course again reflected the round of the Sun thru the 25,920 years of the Great Year of Precession; and both were marked by the Sun's passage thru the twelve signs of zodiacal meaning.

He who interprets the Zodiakos with full intelligibility, will depict the Life of man in all its reaches.

The knowledge of this Astral Script, this Book with Seven Seals (Rev. 5), then the Twelve Great Seals (Rev. 22:2), was imparted in full or in part to the initiate of the Ancient Mysteries.

It is gravely doubtful if any one in this age knows the import of the entire Wheel Of Life, pictured in Tarot Card 10. We catch fragmentary glimpses of its meaning, but the deeper connotation of the symbol eludes the mind. Its profundity is practically fathomless. We can only follow such hints as are given by the archaic sages in their wonderful scriptures.

It is clear, in outline, that the solar year is a precise reflection of the external nature of the Astral Man. It is particularly a vivid typograph of the history of the Ego in and out of incarnation.

The two groups of upper signs of the Zodiakos, the air and fire triplicities, represent, symbolically, the life of the Ego when out of the body in the empyrean. The lower six, the water and earth triplicities, cover the Ego in the watery physical body, hence they are dubbed the six water signs.

The lower six are a reflection or image of the upper six, as water reflects what is above it in the air and light. So, the Life of man below is a reflected counterpart of his Ego above... This is symbolized by the interlaced triangles.

The Ego's journey round the Wheel of Life, thru the alternate realms of incarnate and discarnate life, comprises its cyclical history in this aeon.

As the Macrocosm sets the norm of its life-method by its alternations of day and night in the physical and astral domains, there are seen to be typical of the experience of the Ego in its successive sojourns in the realms of astral "day" and material "night".

The conscious, immortal Ego of man swings endlessly thru the two phases of the Zodiakos, upper and lower, of which circulation the daily and annual phenomenon of the Sun's movements is an exact miniature copy.

The Sun Myth was based solidly on the fact that the Sun is not only the type, but the essential essence of the Ego of man, and that its annual course is graphically pictorial of the Ego's cyclical history.

The Microcosm is a miniature solar universe, a planetary system, comprehended of infinite cells or minor systems; and the Astral Light glowing at the center of his being is the Central Sun of his system.

Contemplate what it would mean for man if the Christian world had a school that taught the Ageless Wisdom of the "superstitious heathens" of the pagan world.

- - - - - - - - - - -

Ouspensky wrote:

When I saw the Sun in the sky, I realized that it is itself the expression of the Fiery Word and that the Emperor was its symbol.

The great luminary shone on the earth and gave it warmth, and the tall golden sunflowers nodded their heads, and all Nature smiled.

And I saw two little children, a boy and a girl, holding hands, in a garden, both naked to show their state of Edenic innocence, and behind them a stone wall of five courses, representing the five human senses which obstruct man's course in life because they deceive more often than not. The Sun showered them with its rays, and it seemed that golden rain was falling upon them.

For an instant I closed my eyes, and when I opened them again, I saw that every ray of the Sun was the scepter of the Emperor, which bore life within it.

And I saw how, beneath the sharp points of the rays, the mystical flowers of the earth were unfolding everywhere, and how the rays penetrated everything, and how all Nature was continually born over and over from the union
of the sun's rays and the earth.

The Philosophers Stone

The Philosopher's Stone dealt with the secret of being always young and
never to die. Such has in all times been the dream of the Alchemists.

To change lead, mercury and all the other metals into gold was a blind
employed to conceal the real secret.

The philosophical gold, in philosophy, is the Absolute. The pursuit of
the Great Work was the Search for the Absolute; and the work itself, was the
work of the Sun.

The Sun was the hieroglyphic sign of Truth, because it is the source of
Light.

Masonry is a search for Light. That search leads us directly back to
the Sun.

The Chaldeans termed the Sun the Father of Light. Hence, the Chaldean
oracle said: "The Father took from Himself, and did not confine His fire
within His intellectual potency. ... All things are begotten from one Fire."

The ancients adored the Sun under the form of a Black Stone, called
Elagabalus, or Heliogabalus.

This Stone is the pure Gold of the Philosopher, and the Philosophal
Stone is the foundation of the Absolute Philosophy, the Supreme and unalter-
able Reason.

The Sun and the Moon of the Alchemist concur in perfecting and giving
stability to the Philosophal Stone.

The Philosophal Stone is the primal means of making the philosophical
gold, that is to say, of transforming all the vital powers of man into the
Sun.

To find the Philosophal Stone is to have discovered the Absolute. The
Absolute is that which admits of no errors, is the Fixed from the Volatile,
is the Law of the Imagination, is the very essence of Being, is the immutable
Law of Truth and Reason.

The Absolute is that which IS. As to man, the Absolute is the Ego.

To find the Absolute in the Infinite, in the Indefinite, and in the Finite, is the Magnum Opus, the Great Work of the Sages, which Hermes called
the Work of the Sun.

To find the immovable base of Philosophal Truth is the secret of Hermes in its entirety, the Philosophal Stone.

He who possesses the Philosophal Stone, possesses the Grand Arcanum and is a cosmic King, and more than a king, for he is inaccessible to all fears and all empty hopes.

THE GOLDEN WHEEL

THE HIEROPHANT

THE MOON.

Chapter XI

CARD 5, THE HIEROPHANT AND CARD 18, THE MOON

Card 5, The Hierophant

Number Five is the most deeply occult of all the digits. Few grasp its full significance and what it represents in their evolution and accomplishment.

5 is the number that symbolizes man in a two-fold aspect. For man stands at the apex of physical evolution, the crowning point of all the lower kingdoms, and midway between 1 and 10.

Man is the universally structured type. In one aspect, all lower types rise toward man and are completed in him. And furthermore, man is the only species that stands erect, with cerebrum positioned at right angles to the spinal column; the only species with a spoken language, an alphabet, a recorded history, and a prospective future.

The number 5, like man's 5th Principle, Mind, is dual. It belongs both to the lower square, the Four Elements, and to the higher triad, illustrated by the equilateral triangle, in which the positive and negative forces from the Dot above, produce a stable manifestation on the physical plane, the base line.

5 refers to the five sacred words, corresponding to the five sacred words of Brahma, said to have been written upon the shining garment of the

gospel Jesus at his "glorification", viz. "Zama Zama Ozza Rachama Ozai", which is translated:

"The robe, the glorious robe of my Strength."

The reality back of this symbol is that number 5 represents the 5 mystic powers which must be attained and manifested thru the Robe of Flesh by every resurrected Initiate after he has passed his three days in the tomb, ere he can attain the Great Initiation.

These five mystic powers are the result of the unfoldment and use of man's five senses upon the inner planes of consciousness.

The use of man's 5 senses in the "man of darkness" is, as it were, covered with a veil, so that only in exceptional cases is one found here and there who is able to extend the functioning of his senses to the inner worlds.

Clairvoyance, while often called the 6th sense, is but the extension of the sense of sight to include the astral world; clairaudience, the extension of hearing; psychometry, the sense of touch, etc., taste and smell being generally omitted.

But this is only drawing aside one corner of the veil; for when man dons the "glorious Robe of his Strength", he finds the functioning of his senses extended as far beyond the astral as the range of a color is extended by the multiplication of its shadings.

And out of the synthesis of all these extended senses, there will be evolved a 6th sense which will be incomprehensible to him who is confined to a more limited use of his senses; and from the development of the 6th sense, a 7th sense will be evolved.

It is to the experiences of these higher worlds, reached momentarily during periods of meditation and contemplation in some instances, that Paul alluded when he said they were "unlawful (i.e., impossible) to utter" or express in words (2 Cor. 12:4).

The body thus glorified thru the 5 powers is called the Robe of Initiation. Unless the Neophyte has donned this Robe, and manifested its powers in the flesh, the Great Initiation has not been passed.

These powers become 7 only after the Robe of Flesh has been laid aside and the Ego has donned the glorious, immortal Body of the Resurrection (Card 20), called the Nirmanakaya Robe, or the Body of the Fire-breath.

In other words, man is the God of Creation when he has woven the 5 mystic powers into his body and donned "the glorious Robe of his Strength."

But when he has donned the Nirmanakaya Robe he has become more than a man.

This should give the student a glimpse of what ultimate Mastery means. But he should not be discouraged; for we see the miracle foreshadowed almost daily in momentary visions of the higher worlds, and we have the prophecy given us in symbolic dreams.

The foregoing statements enlighten somewhat the man of darkness as to the character of the Hierophant, the Master of the Temple of Initiation.

The commentators of the Dark Ages believed this card presented a Pope seated on his throne. The Tarot originated thousands of years before the world ever heard of a Pope.

Hierophant or Mystagog was the title of the chief officer of the Eleusinian Mysteries in Greece. He was the introductor of the novices into the Eleusinian Tmeple, and passed them from the lesser into the greater mysteries, where he became the Demiurg, and impressed the initiate, while teaching him, by his manner and his voice.

The title of Mys-agog was awarded him because he alone revealed the secret or mystery of the phenomenal world, explaining to the initiate the inner import of the external appearance, the world of change, the world of illusion, whereby man is surrounded and the origin of which he does not understand.

In the picture the Hierophant sits on a throne, between two pillars, grey in color, signifying wisdom. The design on the capitals of the pillars is the phallic symbol of union, implying Creation. The two pillars repeat the motive of duality, and suggest the Law of Polarity.

At the back of the throne, on both sides of the Hierophant's head, are two circles with horns, signifying the sign Taurus.

His external robe is red, the color corresponding to Taurus. It has for trimming a border of blue-green, corresponding to the sign Scorpio, the sign opposite Taurus. The outer garment at the neck is caught with a clasp in the form of a lunar crescent, a symbol of the Moon which is exalted in Taurus. Its position at the throat indicates that Taurus rules that part of the body.

Under his red robe appears a garment of blue, like that of the Priestess, and having the same implication. Under this is a white garment, like that of the Fool's, and indicating the same significance.

His crown is a triple tiara, and of gold, symbolizing Solar Radiation and Wisdom. It is ornamented with three rows of trefoils: top row, 3, indicating the three realms, astral, mental, and physical. The middle row, 5, implying the five senses. The bottom row, 7, indicating the seven senses of the Seer.

The crosses on his shoes, the backs of his hands, on the handles of the two keys, and the four on the carpet repeat the symbolism of the ten circular ornaments and crosses on the black robe of the Fool, and represent the four fixed signs of the Zodiakos which form the Solar Cross of Life, which the church changed to the "old rugged cross" of its mythical Christ.

Number 10 is the symbol of unity and completion. Among the Hindus, 10 is referred to as a magic power. The cipher represents the vast field of man's unmanifested powers, which are useless to him except as by his attainment and use of the Rod of Power which the Fool carries on his right shoulder, he brings them into manifestation and gives them their proper place in 10.

In some cases 10 represents the five senses doubled, because of the constant struggle between the lower and higher mind.

Hanging from the crown, behind his ears, is an ornament in the form of a yoke. This refers to the esoteric meaning of the letter Vau, the third letter of J H V H. It falls behind his ears to draw attention to these organs of hearing.

In his left hand he holds erect the triple cross. This is the Rod of Power by which he can penetrate into the three worlds, and rule them, and with poise, equilibrium and calm understanding utilize the powers entrusted to him to bring forth on the three planes -- physical, mental, and astral.

His right hand forms the sign of Esotericism and is raised in blessing over the heads of the two Neophytes kneeling before him. The crown of their heads is shaved to permit freer passage of the Silver Cord (Eccl. 12:6), which penetrates the skull at the Fonticulus Frontalis, and, by condensation, forms the brain, spinal cord and nerve system, as explained by Hotema in "The Flame Divine."

The crossed keys at his feet and the black and white checker-work at the edges of the carpet symbolize the dual phases of Polarity, the Creative Principle.

The symbolism of this card indicates some of the knowledge which the Hierophant imparts to the Neophyte in the ritual of initiation.

He is called the Master of the Temple because he first mastered the Temple in which his Ego dwells in order to become an Initiate and later to rise to the exalted position of Hierophant.

We shall see in Card 16 what happens to him who conquers cities and armies but fails to conquer himself.

The Temples of the Ancient Masters were patterned after the human form, as a study of the ground-plan of either the sanctuary of Karnak, or of Solomon's Temple will prove.

As the Temples of initiation were copies of man's body, the rituals which were given in the various chambers of the Temple were designed to symbolize certain vital processes of the human body.

The possession of the occult keys to human salvation thru self-knowledge was the goal for which the Masters of all ages have labored.

In this modern age, the direction of the quest has changed. The principle task now is to keep man in ignorance in order to make his enslavement the more sure and certain.

The schools, churches, lodges, orders and organizations which pretend to teach useful knowledge, do nothing more than to condition the Mind to accept the standardized systems by which man is surrounded.

The Quintic Quality

The Absolute, Astral Light, Solar Electricity, Cosmic Radiation, forms the Four Elements in its primal condensation. As these Four Elements unite to form man's body, they produce a special organ called Brain, and the function of the brain produces that mysterious Quintic Quality called Mind, the fifth principle which we mentioned above.

When man first appeared on earth, many of the monster animals still were living which inhabit warm regions, as the mammoth, mastodon, saber-tooth tiger, etc.

These huge, ferocious beasts were not afraid of this pigmy that walked upright on two hind legs. To them, he was merely another type of animal, and was a subject for attack and annihilation the same as any other animal.

But in one definite respect this animal was a far different type: He had a powerful ally, which we now call Mind, and still science does not know what it is.

This powerful ally was to make this particular animal supreme over all others, as stated in the Bible (Gen. 1:26), and he lost no time in demonstrating that, while he might be called an animal, he was of a superior type.

The Quintic Quality responsible for man's standing above all other animals is centered in the Golden Bowl (Eccl. 12:6), -- his brain capacity and mental development.

This supreme quality is not the product of evolution. The first men had it as shown by their manufacture of implements of the chase, for defense and offense, in building temples, and in the invention of various symbols which represent cosmic elements, principles and processes, -- symbols so complicated that they cannot today be interpreted by men of high intelligence.

When the Ancient Masters wrote that the Kingdom of the God is within you (Luke 17:21), they referred to the Mind.

All standardized systems of education and religion are designed to condition and control the Mind.

When we control the Mind, we control the man. When we bind the Mind, we bind the man.

The ever-watchful church has used, and still uses, every psychological trick to control the Mind of the masses.

In our Mind we build a God, endow him with all the glorious and powerful qualities we can imagine, and then set out to find him, -- and we lose him. He vanishes like a fog before the morning sunshine.

Luther said: "God is a blank tablet, on which there is nothing save that which thou thyself hast written."

Naquet wrote: "Whenever knowledge takes a step forward, God recedes a step backward."

Card 18, The Moon

In our review of Card 19, the Sun, we saw the substance of the teaching the neophyte got concerning the nature of Life and the constitution of Man. Now we shall see the part the Moon plays, according to Ancient Science.

We have noted that the six lower signs of the Zodiakos, the water and the earth triplicities, represent the Ego in the watery physical body. This is the phase of Life that is symbolized by the Moon.

The Moon was the ancient symbol of physical man, since the body, the physical and emotional, were the products of a precedent evolution on the Moon.

According to Astrology, the Sun and the Moon, in their interaction each lunar month, performed the whole drama of human evolution with such graphic fidelity, that the delineation of it becomes a perpetual marvel.

No graphology of mythicism has ever excelled Nature herself in the vivid portrayal of the dual history of man upon the very face of the Moon, where the story, eternally repeated, has been enacted before the eyes of successive generations of mortals, but never interpreted since the days of ancient Egypt.

On the other hand, this phase of Life has been bitterly condemned by the Mother Church as the stupid, unfounded belief of "superstitious heathens."

This position of course has been imperative for the church in order to conceal the source of its ridiculous religious system.

In the various phases and aspects of the registration of the Sun's light upon its body, the Moon stages the entire symbolical drama of the bledeed physico-astral Life of mortal man with a precision so astonishing, that the human mind which once follows the analogies, cannot escape the conviction that Cosmic Intelligence presided at the directing of the movements of the Sun, the Moon and the Earth in their interrelation.

This phase of the subject is understood by those who have read with unprejudiced intelligence Hotema's work titled "Cosmic Creation," in which it is shown that all these bodies originally evolved from a gigantic cloud of Astral Dust.

As seen from the earth, the Sun and the Moon, together, depict in the sky each month, the record of man's typical Life so fully, that it becomes a prime enigma to account for the loss of the Wisdom to interpret this Astral Phenomenon after it had once been known.

The rejection and destruction of the Arcane Science by the Church, cost the Christian world the forfeiture of its ability to read this elementary text-book of Astrology, with its record written in characters of alternate light and darkness.

As the Ego was born periodically in the physical world, so the Sun was reborn monthly in the Moon, matter's planetary symbol.

We find that both Horus and Khunsu; the two Egyptian characters which represented the renewed Solar God, were depicted in the disk of the full Moon.

The Egyptian planisphere of Denderah shows the two astral bodies in this position.

Khunsu's father was Amen, the "hidden god", the youthful Khunsu being his visible representative, reborn in the New Moon.

Horus was the renewed Ra, Osiris or Atum. And that character which, in solar symbolism, was reborn in the vernal equinox or the eastern rim of the morning, was re-dramatized in lunar symbolism as finding rebirth in the young crescent Moon.

Osiris, Atum or Ra, sinking in apparent feebleness and death in the cycle of the waning Moon, came to their renaissance at nightfall, between the two horns of the crescent in the west, symbolized in the Crown of the High Priestess in Card 2.

The Moon repeated thirteen times in a year the death and resurrection story, while the Sun traced it once. So, the thirteen Yods in Card 19, the Sun, are placed six on each side of the picture, and one between the heads of the boy and the girl.

Ages of intelligence have gazed upon this monthly astrological drama without once descrying its tacit narrative. Yet, the ancient Egyptians discoursed in chapter after chapter on the profound meaning of this phenomenon.

Shall we conclude that ancient eyes penetrated deeper into cosmic secrets than modern?

The evidence is beofre us, but the conclusion should not be founded on a false premise. For fifteen hundred years it meant burning at the iron stake for him who was so indiscreet as to present any knowledge of astrological phenomena.

Now this datum may be resurrected since it has become safer to present knowledge of this character, and again become the bulwark of the Ageless Wisdom, rendering it impregnable to theological and materialistic assault.

While books and Bibles may be brushed aside with scorn by science, the chart of man's astral constitution, written ineradicably upon the open sheet of the nightly sky, cannot be gainsaid. For here is an indelible scripture, whose ever-turning pages must be read alike by the theist and the atheist.

Here is a cosmic record that no mind dare flout. For here are the heavens themselves preaching a cosmic sermon and reciting a gospel narrative that no mortal can contemn.

The Shining Moon at night is the symbol, representative, vice-regent of the Sun when it is buried in darkness. The Moon holds the proxy of its power. It is the transmitter of Solar Light when the Sun is out of sight. It is the only witness of the Sun's light when the Sun is unable to shine on that part of the earth.

The Moon is the Sun by night. When the Sun is in full panoply in the sky of day, the Moon is eclipsed. But she comes into her glory in the night.

The Moon stands between man and total darkness, yet she has no light of her own to give. She simply reflects the brightness of one higher than herself.

And here we have the two great cosmic characters in the ancient drama, with man as the spectator and interpreter, and, as he realizes to his amazement, the ultimate actor.

Intelligent meaning begins to appear as soon as we have fixed in their respective roles the two chief dramatis personae.

The Sun and the Moon, according to ancient Astrology, perform the parts of man's Ego and his body respectively, and their interaction, so skilfully portrayed by the Astrologers, will be found to depict in detail the connected history of the two, on the earth and in the body.

In some pictures of Card 18, a wolf and a dog appear on eaither side of the Path of Life leading up from the stream.

In Tarot Cards at the Bibliotheque Nationale of Paris, under the name of the Tarot of Charles VI, these two animals do not appear, being replaced by two astrologers who are studying the Moon.

Concerning Card 18, Ouspensky wrote:

"I saw a desolate plain stretched out before me. The full Moon looked down as if wrapped in meditation. Under her wavering light the shadows lived their own peculiar lives. There were black hills on the distant horizon.

"Between two grey towers wound the Path of Life extending up from a stream. It faded out in the distance, and I saw two strange men who were studying the Moon. From the stream a great, black crayfish crawled up on to the bank.

"The Path of Life, rising and falling with the undulating terrain, had been worn by the feet of the many mortals who had traveled it before me. In the foreground it traversed a cultivated field, symbolizing things of common knowledge, until it came to the two towers, which marked the limit of the known. From there it went into the region of the unknown.

"A cold, heavy dew was falling, and a feeling of dread overcame me. I felt the presence of a mysterious world, a world of hostile elements, of corpses rising from the grave, of tormented ghosts.

"In the pale light of the Moon I seemed to feel the presence of phantoms; shadows seemed to be crossing the path; someone was waiting for me behind the towers -- and it was dangerous to look back."

In the sunset of life, in this world of fraud, when the step begins to falter and the Silver Threads begin to appear among the Gold, phantoms appear in the Mind of the man of darkness, shadows of the unknown obscure the Path of Life, and one hopes that one's loved ones, who have been "born again" and preceded one to the Astral World, will be waiting to welcome one beyond the towers.

THE LOVERS.

THE STAR.

Chapter XII

CARD 6, TEMPTATION & CARD 17, THE STAR

Card 6, Temptation (The Lovers)

In this picture the glorious Sun, Father of Light and Giver of Life, shines in the zenith.

Beneath the Sun is Mikael, one of the Four Great Angels of the Solar God, with arms extended, pouring down the blessings of Life upon two human figures in the foreground beneath the Angel, male and female, unveiled, apparently representing Adam and Eve in the Edenic Garden.

We are now at the threshold of the ancient fable concerning Humanity, and are facing all the mythology that was invented by the Masters and woven around Man, the God of the physical world, the greatest and most perfect organization of astral substance known, and still a mystery to science.

Behind the man is the Edenic Tree of Life, bearing twelve fiery fruits, and mentioned in the Bible (Rev. 22:2). The twelve fruits are intended to represent the twelve signs of the Zodiakos. Each fruit has triple flames, as the astrologers subdivided each sign into three parts, or decantes.

Behind the woman is the Edenic Tree of the Knowledge of Good and Evil, bearing five fruits, which are intended to symbolize the Five Senses which rule humanity and make man a prisoner in a physical jail. Around this Tree is entwined the Evil Serpent of Sensuality.

Various commentators have called this card The Lovers, Marriage, and Temptation. We adopt the latter term as it agrees with the ancient fable.

Some pseudo-occultists call this picture "The Two Paths," and say that older versions of the symbolism show a man standing between two women, who represent Virtue and Vice respectively.

This refers to the Two Paths mentioned in the Bible. The strait and narrow Path winds uphill all the way to the Realm of Seership. The other is the broad road that leads to destruction, and many there be who go in thereat (Mat. 7:13).

In older exoteric versions of the Tarot, there are three figures, a youth, a maiden, and a crowned woman. These are the Kabalistic Son and Bride and the Kabalistic Mother.

Our version is essentially the same as that of Dr. A. E. Waite, and is based upon the unpublished esoteric Tarot.

In the Bible two Serpents are mentioned. One Good and one Evil. The Serpent of Sensuality is the Evil One. The Good Serpent is the White Serpent of the Caduceus.

These two Serpents represent many things. Later in the New Testament they appear in the form of the Two Thieves who were crucified with the gospel Jesus, as stated by Hotema in "Son of Perfection."

In that instance the Evil one "railed on Jesus", and was rebuked by the Good one (Lu. 23:39, 40).

The Good Serpent represents the Wisdom and Liberation resulting from the rightful adaptation of the very forces which, at first, tempt us into wrongful action that leads to destruction.

The woman, in her weakness, looks toward the Angel. The man, in his boldness, looks toward the woman. The attitude of the woman appears as an appeal for help to resist the powerful urge of animalistic generation. That of the man appears as inviting lust.

In the present stage of evolution, the existence and continuance of the race depends primarily on woman, causing her to be more fully under the influence of the Law of Generation than man.

It is one of man's primary duties to help woman in her struggle against the strong urge of the Law. But man has failed miserably, and as a result, "cursed is the ground for thy sake" (Gen. 3:17).

Humanal improvement is utterly impossible until man graduates in the conquest of his body by subduing his animalistic nature. The results of his failure are presented in cards 12, 15, and 16.

The student will find much help on this point by reading Hotema's work "Great Red Dragon," and that remarkable debate on "The Virgin Birth" in 1936 between Dr. H. M. Shelton and Dr. G. R. Clements, published by Health Research.

Card 17, The Star

Our interpretation of some of the Tarot cards varies much from that of other commentators, because we observe the philosophy of those who invented and designed the pictures.

The interpretation of the symbolism will not present the views of the Masters who made them unless it agrees with the basic principles of their philosophy.

We have considered Card 19, The Sun, and Card 18, The Moon, and have now reached Card 17, The Star, and shall show how these three astral bodies were directly connected in the life of man by the Ancient Astrologers.

According to ancient folk-tradition, man's original home was in the Sun, whence he "fell" with the loss of his divine prerogative, first to the Moon, and thence to the earth, where he became the Great Star under certain conditions.

The Ancient Astrologers listed Seven Grades of Being as represented in the human microcosm, the four lower pertaining to the phenomenal order, while the three upper ones, (1) higher manas or abstract intellect, (2) buddhi or intuition, and (3) Atma or pure Ego, are noumenal and immortal.

The super-phenomenal triad was symbolized in the ancient philosophy by the Sun. So, the journey to the Sun was nothing more nor less than a symbolic designation of the process of rendering fully actual, the latent potentialities of these three transcendent microcosmic principles.

Similarly, the journey to the Moon designated the much less arduous attainment of the highest grade of merely natural evolution, so far at least as humanal and physical denizens of the solar system are concerned.

Now, these two goals, "sun", and "moon", correspond respectively to the King's and Queen's Chambers in the Great Pyramid of Gizeh, accepting the current identification of this structure as a Temple of Initiation.

When these two goals are attained during physical life, man passes into a segment of the Wheel Of Life which only a few human beings ever traverse. It is the result of the concomitant energization of two little-known and little-understood cerebral structures, known as the Pineal Gland, which Descartes identified as the point of contact between brain and Ego, and the Pituitary Gland.

Now, in hieroglyphical language, a Star always denoted a God in the ancient philosophy; and a God is a man who possesses supernal powers, a Seer.

This great radiant Star has eight points, its geometrical formation being similar to that of the Wheel Of Life, Card 10, and the symbols of the Ego embroidered on the vesture of the Fool.

The seven lesser Stars which surround the Great Star also have eight rays, and we shall see in due time what they represent.

The summary of several tawdry explanations say that this is a card of

Hope. Some term it a symbol of Prudence. On other planes it has been certified as Immortality and Interior Light. We shall see that the last two are correct.

The woman in the foreground is naked. Her left knee rests on the land and her right foot on the water. She pours water from two vessels, one of gold and one of silver. This is said by some to represent the Water of Life, and this is correct (Rev. 22:1).

Some commentators believe the woman is Hathor, or Mother Nature. In some respects she may be identified with the High Priestess, and also with the Empress. Dr. A. E. Waite calls her the Great Mother in the Kabalistic Sephira Binah, which is Supernal Understanding, and this is correct.

The bird on a bush in the picture is a scarlet Ibis, the Egyptian bird sacred to Hermes. Being perched on a bush, some say it represents the brain and nerve system, and we shall see that this is correct.

Book With Seven Seals

In considering Card 2, High Priestess, we referred to the Book with Seven Seals mentioned in the Bible.

One commentator, coming closer than the rest, while not understanding the secret of the Great Star, said the seven smaller stars symbolize the "seven interior stars" of the body.

These centers of the body are called the Seven Chakras in Hindu literature, and are listed in the following order:

1. Muladhara, the Sacral Plexus
2. Svadishthana, the Prostatic Plexus
3. Manipura, the Solar Plexus
4. Anahata, the Cardiac Plexus
5. Vishiddha, the Pharyngeal Plexus
6. Ajna, the Pituitary Gland in the Brain
7. Sahasrara, the Pineal Gland of the Brain

Had that commentator followed this trail further, he had found the ancient secret of the Great Star.

Hotema has covered these chakras in his "Son of Perfection" and we shall here notice in particular the last two.

6. The Ajna chakra is the astral center of the region of the forehead between the eyebrows. It is a lustrous moon-white in color, shining with a mystic, trance-like glory.

7. The Sahasrara is situated in the crown of the head and termed the "dwelling place of Shiva. ... In the inner center there is the mystic Great Void worshipped by the Devas in secret."

Quoting further: "It is in the Sahasrara that the negative (female) creative force, Kundalini Shakti, meets and unites with the positive principle (male) after its ascent from the Sacral Plexus.

-99-

"He who has known the Great Void in the Sahasrara is freed from rebirths (reincarnation). He cannot be bound in any of the three worlds, and can travel the sky at will" (Kundalini Power, Pandit Drishtva).

The Ineffable Name, J. H. V. H, is directly related to these occult mysteries, and in particular, to the Four Principal Glands of the body primarily involved in Generation, as follows:

1. Pineal, solar center in the brain.
2. Pituitary, aeriferous center in the brain.
3. Prostate, Water of Life (Semen) center of the body.
4. Gonads, animalistic procreation center of the body.

Astral Light

The ancient philosophy tells us that when the Water of Life is conserved for the body's use, and not consumed in generation, it then flows up the spinal cord as the "Nibodhika" Fire, energizing in its upward flow the Seven Nerve Plexuses above mentioned. As a result, the whole body, according to the Bible, is filled with Astral Light (Mat. 6:22).

The Bible says, "Take heed therefore that the (Astral) Light which is in thee be not darkness (because of its being consumed in fornication and generation).

"If thy whole body therefore be full of (Astral) Light, having no part of dark, the whole (body) shall be full of (Astral) Light, as when the bright shining of a candle doth give thee Light" (Lu. 11:35, 36).

These statements make sense when they are correctly understood.

The peculiar effects of these profound biological processes, about which modern science knows nothing, are described in symbol and parable in verses 12-17 of Chapter 6, and in Chapters 7 - 11 of the last book of the Bible.

Not a minister in Christendom nor a doctor of medicine is competent to interpret the symbolism and allegories in Revelation which refer to these things, for they know not the nature of Life nor the constitution of Man.

That symbolism and these allegories deal not with gods and saviors as taught by the church, but with the Living Fire in Man, centered at the base of the spinal column, which may be divided horizontally into three sections, the lowest including the lumbar vertebrae, together with the segments forming the sacrum and coccyx.

The lowest area is surrounded by a dull red haze, oily in texture and lurid in color. Higher up the color grows lighter and becomes orange.

Thru these spinal sections composed of the twelve dorsal vertebrae, there is a golden glow radiating from a thread-like line that appears as a tiny river of Golden Fire.

These deep anatomical and physiological secrets, unknown to modern science, are described in the Bible as "two golden pipes (which) empty the golden oil out of themselves" (Zech. 4:12).

Still higher the golden color fades to yellow, becoming tinged with a light green. Thru the cervical section of the spinal cord the color of the oil becomes faintly electric blue.

Thru the "two golden pipes", called the Ida and Pingala nadis by the Hindus, this Astral Stream of Living Fire flows incessantly up and down.

These "two golden pipes" are also the Two Serpents of the Caduceus. They are the "two thieves" that were crucified with the gospel Jesus. They are the "two witnesses", the "two olive trees", and the "two candlesticks" mentioned in the Bible, and described in detail by Hotema in "Son of Perfection."

The farther up the Living Fire flows, the thinner and fainter is its hue, but the purer the colors, until finally the dual streams of the "two golden pipes" converge in a seething mass in the pons of the medulla oblongata of the brain, the function of which science knows nothing.

At this point a strange biological process occurs, practically unknown to the modern world. The Astral Fire now begins to permeate the third ventricle of the brain and to stimulate the Pituitary Gland.

Marriage of the Lamb

We have noticed the Pituitary and Pineal glands of the brain, concerning the functions of which modern science knows very little about the former and nothing at all as to the latter.

The Pituitary is the negative, passive, female pole of the body, yet it plays an important part in the development of the body and mind.

The Ancient Masters, being aware of these things, called the Pituitary the Builder of the Temple. In the Bible it is symbolized as Zerubbabel (Zech. 4:9), and preachers think this Zerubbabel was some great architect.

From the Bible we quote: "For who hath despised the day of small things? For they shall rejoice, and shall see the plummet in the hand of Zerubabble with those seven; they are the eyes of the Lord, which run to and fro thru the whole earth" (Zech. 4:10).

The "seven eyes" are the Seven Nerve Plexuses mentioned above, and the whole earth represents man's body. The plummet represents the waves of Astral Fire which we shall soon mention.

The Pituitary, as the Builder of the Human Temple, is the initiator in the function of man's higher mental development; for it "resurrects" the candidate (Pineal) from the semi-dormant state in the average man.

Being of feminine polarity, the Pituitary performs true to its dignity by being the eternal Temptress. Manly Hall said:

"In the Egyptian myth, Isis, who partakes of the nature of the Pituitary, conjures Ra (who represents the Sun and here is symbolical of the Pineal) to disclose his secret name, which he finally does. The Physiological process (of this disclosure) is worthy of consideration."

As the rising Astral Fire stimulates the Pituitary, it "begins to glow and little rippling rings of (Astral) Light flow out from around it and gradually fade out a short distance away.

"As the stimulation continues....the emanating rings around the gland grow stronger. They are not equally distributed. The circles are elongated on the side facing the third ventricle (of the brain) and extend out in graceful parabolas toward the Pineal gland.

"Gradually, as the current grows stronger, the circles approaching ever closer to the slumbering eye of Shiva (Pineal), tinting the Pineal with golden light and gently coaxing it into activity.

"Under the benign warmth and radiance of the Pituitary fire, the divine eye thrills and flickers, and the mystery of occult unfoldment occurs." -- Melchizedek and the Mystery of Fire.

H. P. Blavatsky phrases this part of the process in these words:

"The arc (of Light) from the Pituitary mounts upward more and more toward the Pineal, until the (electric) current striking it, as when an electric current strikes some solid object, the dormant (Pineal) gland is activated and set all aglowing with the akashic (Astral) fire."

This is the golden secret of the Great Star. Its region is man's brain. In most cases it is semi-dormant. When resurrected by the Astral Fire, it fills the whole body full of Light, says the Bible.

That exalted state is attained by bridging the gap between the Pituitary and Pineal, which then establishes direct connection between the objective and subjective departments of Consciousness, raising man up to the sublime state of Seership.

So, the Great Star symbolizes Seership in the ancient philosophy.

The Seven Smaller Stars represent the Seven Sense Powers of the Seer.

All the stars in the picture have eight points. This symbolizes many things in human life. We shall notice some of them.

Eight is the Number of Evolution and is connected with the spiral motion of cycles.

At the end of the seventh cycle, the primary phase of the creation of the earth was completed, and the second phase began.

The eighth note in music is a repetition of the first, but in a higher octave. It is the beginning of a higher cycle.

Eight is the number of the inevitable and onward rush of Time. Its symbol is the hour-glass and the balance. It is also the Winged Globe of Egypt, and the Bird of Life, the Scarlet Ibis, which was sacred to Hermes.

The bird in the picture of Card 17 sets on a nearby bush, and the Egyptians symbolized it as carrying man up from the earth plane, the lower o of

the 8, to the astral plane, the upper o of the 8, where he enters a higher
cycle and becomes a Sage, a Perfected Personality, one with the Universe of
Being.

This higher stage, said Blavatsky, "is the psycho-physiological illustration of these two organs on the physical plane which are the concrete symbols of the metaphysical concepts called Manas and Buddhi."

The latter, to attain consciousness on the earth level, needs the more
differentiated Fire of Manas. But Manas is deprived of that Fire when it is
consumed at the spinal base of the body in fornication and generation.

So, it seems that man may have progeny or seership, but not both. He
must sacrifice the one to gain the other under the law of compensation.

This is the esoteric meaning of the biblical statement that "blood" must
be shed for the remission of sin (Mat. 26:28).

Paul said, "Almost all things are by the law (of compensation and evolution) purged with blood; and without shedding of blood is no remission"
(Heb. 9:22).

The actual meaning of these biblical allegories becomes clear when the
basic principles are known and understood.

These allegorical statements do not mean the nailing of a god to a
cross.

Christianity is a base fraud that was invented by the personalization
of ancient symbols and the literalization of ancient allegories. Then the
scrolls were destroyed to conceal the facts.

When man consumes the Solar Fire in generation, he is blessed with children as his reward. By denying himself that earthly pleasure, he gains by
rising to the exalted plane of Seership under the guidance of a Guru.

When the Sixth Principle, Manas, Pituitary, has energized the Seventh,
Buddhi, Pineal, the Astral Fire, flowing from the latter, "illuminates the
field of infinitude", wrote Blavatsky. And she added:

"For that period of time, Man becomes omniscient; the Past and Future,
Space and Time, disappear (as in dreams), and for him becomes the Present."

So, the great Carrel said: "For the Clairvoyant there are no secrets."

And the Bible states: "There is nothing covered, that shall not be revealed (to such man); and nothing hid, that shall not be known" (Mat. 10:26).

Dr. Charles Whitby sums up the secret in these words:

"Thus the journey to the 'moon' is equated with the consummation of
psycho-mental development, and the consequent psychic energization of the
Pituitary.

"And thence the journey to the "Sun" with the activation of the Pineal (involving noumenal illumination); and the 'sparking' process between the two organs with the Hermetic Marriage of the Sun and Moon, or Hermes and Aphrodite, or Ra and Isis" (Back to the Sun).

In the Bible this is termed "the marriage of the Lamb", and the church represents this to mean the marriage of Jesus and the Church. More theological hogwash and hokum to deceive the masses.

This phase of our subject is noticed again under Card 14, TIME.

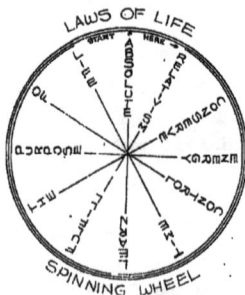

THE CHARIOT.

THE TOWER.

Card 7, The Chariot

Most commentators have failed to interpret the true symbolism of this card. They think it represents the King in his triumph, typifying the victory that creates kingship as its logical consequence and not the vested royalty.

These commentators have missed the Royal Path Of Life, and failed to recollect that the Ancient Masters were not interested in conquering countries, but in conquering the human body.

The Conqueror stands boldly erect in a chariot having the form of a cube stone, representing the earth, with a starry canopy over him, representing the astral world, supported by four pillars, representing the four elements.

This is the same man we saw in Card 0, The Fool. Now we see him again, in his progress to that stage of life where he thinks he is the Conqueror because he has subdued armies, cities, and even nations. We shall later see him at the end of his earthly wanderings, where Justice has passed sentence upon him, Card 11, and the Judgment has been executed, Card 12.

The Conqueror is crowned, and the crown is surmounted by three pentagrams. The pentagram signifies the five senses, and three are shown to indicate the sense power of the average man reaches three planes, the physical, mental, and astral.

In the time of Solomon the breastplate was double, or composed of two

-105-

pieces, forming a kind of purse or bag, in which the Urim and Thummim, symbols of Light and Truth, were enclosed.

Prof. Plumptre supposed the Urim to have been a clear, colorless stone, set in the breastplate of the High Priest as a symbol of Light, answering to the mystic scarab in the pectoral plate of the ancient Egyptian Priests, and that the Thummim was an image corresponding to that worn by the priestly judges of Egypt as a symbol of Truth and Purity of motive. By gazing steadfastly on these, he may have been thrown into a half ecstatic state akin to hypnotism, in which he lost all personal consciousness and received astral illumination and insight.

In the picture the Urim and Thummim are represented by a lunar crescent on each shoulder of the charioteer.

In his right hand the charioteer holds a scepter surmounted by the figure 8, combined with a crescent. This is a combination of the symbol over the Magician's head, with the lunar crown of the Priestess, which signifies the relationship of the Macrocosm and the Microcosm.

The shield on the front of the chariot with a red emblem on it, is one form of the Hindu lingam-yoni,   fying union of the positive and negative forces of Polarity.

Above the shield is the winged-globe of the Egyptians, symbol of the immortal flight of the Ego thru the infinitude of space and time.

A square on his cuirass represents the four elements solidified. On it are three T-squares, symbolizing the three planes mentioned above.

In some Tarot cards the chariot is drawn by two horses, while sphinxes are shown in others, and are attributed by some to an innovation suggested Eliphas Levi.

The colors of the sphinxes are the same as those of the two pillars of the High Priestess, one white and the other black, symbolizing the positive and negative phases of the Creative Principle.

The Charioteer's golden belt suggests Astral Light and the Zodiakos. It is ornamented with the signs of the Zodiakos, and its slanting position suggests the slanting circle of the ecliptic, representing Time and the ences of the astrological bodies.

This card symbolizes in general the main characteristics of the sacred septenary. It represents man who has become the Conqueror, but the planes of his conquest are manifest or external, and not within himself.

If the Conqueror came to the pillars of the Temple between which is seated the High Priestess, he could neither open the scroll called Tora, nor answer the questions she would ask him.

Everything about the charioteer suggests that he summarizes all the powers and potencies of the personages who have preceded him in the series of Major Trumps. He is their synthesis.

Ouspensky wrote:

"I saw a chariot drawn by two sphinxes, a white one and a black one. Four pillars supported a sky-blue canopy, spangled with five pointed stars.

"Beneath the canopy, driving the sphinxes, stood the Conqueror, in steel armour, and in his hand was a scepter surmounted with a figure 8 and a lunar crescent

"Three golden pentagrams shown on his crown. On the front of the chariot, above the sphinxes, was a two-winged sphere, and the mystic lingam and yoni, the symbol of unition.

" 'Everything in this picture has a meaning', said the Voice to me. 'Look and try to understand.

" 'This is the Conqueror who has not yet conquered himself. Here are will and knowledge. But in all this, there is more in the desire to attain, than in real attainment.

" 'The Charioteer began to consider himself conqueror before he actually conquered. He decided that conquest must come to a conqueror. In this there are many possibilities, but also many deceiving lights, and great dangers await the man in the chariot.

" 'He drives the chariot by the strength of his will and of the magic scepter. But the tension of his will may weaken and the sphinxes may pull in different directions and tear him and his chariot asunder.

" 'This is the Conqueror against whom the conquered (body's passions) may still rise. Look behind him at the Towers of the conquered city. Perhaps the flame of revolt burns therein already. (body's passions rebelling against suppression).

" 'And he knows not that within himself lies the city to be conquered; that within himself the sphinxes (positive and negative forces) are watching his every movement, and that within himself great dangers await him.

" 'And realize this is the same man you saw who tripped gaily along with light step as if the earth and its traps held no terrors for him, and paused at the brink of a deep precipice where the crocodile awaited him, but without noticing the beast.' "

The number 7 is the most sacred of all numbers and was so considered by the Ancient Masters.

H. P. Blavatsky wrote: "Number 7 is the festival day of all the earth, the birthday of the world. I know not whether anyone would be able to celebrate the number 7 in adequate terms." -- Secret Doctrine.

All ancient mystery teachings agree that Creation produced the manifested universe thru the Astral Progenitors of the 7 Creative Rays or Hierarchies which constitute the manifested aspect of Supreme Intelligence centered in the cosmic Substance of which all things are made, as explained by Hotema in Cosmic Creation.

Volumes of fables have been woven around the number 7 in connection with the numerous mysteries linked to the work of Cosmic Creation, most of which are nothing more than fairy tales told to children, and were invented to deceive the masses.

Fundamentally, it is said that at the end of the seventh cycle, the primary phase of the creation of the earth was completed, and the second phase began. And just as in the case of music, where the eighth note of the scale is simply a repetition of the first, but in a higher octave, the beginning of a higher cycle.

The original designers of the Tarot applied this law of 7 to man. In Card 7 man appears as the Charioteer, the Conqueror. He has finished the first cycle and is entering the second. It is the number to which the Kabalists assign the idea of Victory. But what has man conquered?

The geometrical symbol of 7 is the interlaced triangles with the Dot in the center, the Dot being the same germinal point that appears within the circle, or the creative nucleus of the mundane egg which has evolved during the six-day-periods of creation thru nature and man, and becomes the synthesized focal point of the forces of its 6 manifestations.

The seventh Sephira is called Netzach, "Firmness and Victory," corresponding to the Ineffable Name J H V H. Hence, man can evolve intellectually to a point where he can unfold the Six Sephira, that is, he can Intertwine the astral attributes with the physical and thus become the magic symbol of Solomon's Seal, the Six Pointed Star, the Seal of Wisdom.

But until man has unfolded or manifested the 7th point and gained complete victory; until he has fixed his gaze upon the Great Star of the Seer, and made that the center from which all his works proceed, he may be a magician with mighty power, but he is not accepted as a White Magician.

- - - - - - - - - - -

It appears inexplicable that none of the commentators on the Tarot discovered the ancient myth of the Charioteer.

In the myth, Clymene, daughter of Oceanus and Tethys and wife of Iapetus, to whom she bore Atlas, Prometheus, and others, became the mother of Phaethon by Helios, the Sun.

Phaethon requested his father to let him drive the Chariot of the Sun across the sky for one day. Helios was induced by the pleas of his son and his mother, Clymene, to yield.

But the youth lacked the strength and skill required to handle the horses, and they rushed out of their regular path, coming so close to the earth that it had been set on fire, had he not been struck with lightning by Jupiter and hurled headlong into the river Eridanus.

The "earth" represents man's body. The Chariot of the Sun indicates the

Solar Fire seething in his body. This "Fire" he must control and successfully negotiate the Circle of the Zodiakos (Cycle of Life) by the development of his 7 principles and 7 powers, and rise to the plane of Seership, Card 17, the Star.

Otherwise, the fate of those who live on the low animalistic level is certain to be the same as was Phaethon's. For, like him, in the circle of the Zodiakos they must face all the monsters, especially Scorpion, which caused the disaster to Phaethon.

The ancient legend said: "Here the Scorpion extended its two great arms, with its tail and crooked claws stretching over two signs of the Zodiakos" (Virgo and Scorpio, which were formerly one sign and represented in ancient magic as Good and Evil, considered in Cards 8 and 15).

"When Phaethon (symbol of the man of darkness) beheld Scorpio reeking with poison and menacing with its fangs, his courage failed and the reins fell from his hands."

This phase of Scorpio symbolizes the test of Sexuality, the great Temptation, and is thus fitly described.

Under this test the self-styled gods and conquerors in mortal fame fail. They have not mastered their own animalistic nature. And, as with Phaethon, the fiery steeds of carnal thought run away with them, and they are dashed to earth.

BOOK WITH SEVEN SEALS

In the last book of the Bible mention is made of the Book with Seven Seals.

This refers to the Charioteer, and describes in symbol and allegory the development of man's 7 principles and his 7 powers on earth, by means of which he rises to the Plane of Seership (Card 17, the Star).

I saw on the right hand of him that sat on the throne a book written within and on the back-side, sealed with seven seals.

And I saw a strong angel proclaiming with a loud voice, Who is worthy to open the book, and to loose the seals thereof?

And no man in heaven, nor in earth, neither under the earth, was able to open the book, neither to look thereon.

And I wept much, because no man was found worthy to open and to read the book, neither to look thereon.

And one of the elders saith unto me, Weep not. Behold, the Lion (Aries, head sign of the Zodiakos), he of the tribe of Juda, the root of David, hath prevailed to open the book, and to loose the seven seals thereof.

And I beheld, and, lo, in the midst of the throne of the four beasts (four fixed signs of the Zodiakos), stood a Lamb as if it had been sacrificed (the trembling neophyte prepared for the ordeal of initiation), having 7 horns (7 powers of noetic action), and 7 eyes (7 noetic perceptive faculties), which are the 7 Breaths of the Macrocosm sent forth into all the earth.

Thus, the symbolical Lamb represents the neophyte who has been prepared for, and is about to undergo the initiatory ordeals, and join the ranks of those who rise to the plane of Seership, the Great Star.

But few there be who travel this strait and narrow path, and the next Card, 16, describes in ancient symbolism the calamity that befalls those who fail to conquer their animalistic nature.

Card 16, The Tower

This card has several titles, among them being "The Lightning-struck Tower," "The Fire of Heaven," "Castle of Plutus," and "The Tower of Babel." In the latter case, the two human figures falling from the Tower are said to be Nimrod and his minister.

The decipherers of the ancient cryptograms have failed to present reasonable and logical interpretations of this card because they have envisioned it in the wrong light.

The Tower has been mentioned as symbolical of the chastisement of pride of the intellect overwhelmed in the attempt to penetrate the "Mystery of God."

The Tower in this picture is struck by lightning, its crown knocked off, with fire blazing from the top, and a man and a woman are falling head-first toward the ground.

These are the same man and woman we saw in Card 6, Temptation, and we shall see them again in Card 15, Evil.

The puzzling symbolism of this card is readily solved by referring to the Bible, and changing the word Tower to Temple.

The Bible calls the human body the Temple of God. And, as that Temple, man towers high above all other animals, with his feet resting upon the earth and his head high up in the Astral World.

The Tower is a very fitting and appropriate symbol of Man.

Man is the driver of the Chariot of the Sun, which means the Solar Spark of his Body. But he fails to develop the strength to direct its power in the higher path.

of his Body. But he fails to develop the strength to direct its power in the higher path.

The logical result is that the Tower (man) is "struck with lightning," as described in the decipherment of the symbolism of Card 7, and the Charioteer is "hurled headlong into the river Eridanus," -- a winding constellation in the southern hemisphere, also called the River of Orion by the Ancient Astrologers.

This "river" is shown in Tarot Card 13 of some sets, which picture a skeleton with a scythe, reaping living hands, feet and heads, which protrude

-110-

from the ground. Behind him is a river flowing toward a setting sun.

The Bible explains why the "Tower is struck with lightning." Here is that explanation:

"Flee fornication. Every sin that man doeth is without the body; but he who committeth fornication sinneth against his own body" (1 Cor. 6:18).

Know ye not that ye are the Temple (Tower) of Astral Light, and that Astral Light dwelleth within you?

If any man defile the Temple (Tower), him shall Astral Lightning destroy; for the Temple (Tower) of Astral Light is holy, which Temple (Tower) ye are (1 Cor. 3:16, 17).

The verses from 5 to 24 of the 7th chapter of Romans are devoted to a discussion that refers to the commandment in the second chapter of Genesis, 17th verse, not to eat of the "forbidden fruit."

The last book of the Bible deals exclusively, in symbol and allegory, with the Temple (Tower) of Astral Light, its seven major nerve centers, and certain of its functions, but chiefly with certain phases of the creative function which are still unknown to medical art and modern science.

These symbols and allegories have been interpreted by Hotema in his work titled "Son of Perfection."

Man is told in Revelation that he who overcometh the animalistic function of generation; and thus refrain from eating of the "forbidden fruit," shall inherit all things good in life (Rev. 21:7).

Blessed are they that obey this commandment, that they may have right to the Tree of Life, but abuse it not (Rev. 22:14).

The River of Life and the two Trees of Life mentioned in the Bible (Rev. 22:1, 2), correspond to the three nadies of the body mentioned in Hindu literature.

But, whereas in the physical body (Temple, Tower) the triple current of Life flowing thru the three nadies ascends to the brain from the base of the spine, from the generative centers, in the Astral Body the "accursed" function, sexuality, does not exist (Rev. 22:3), and the Force of Creative Life flows from above.

In the inverted Ego, which means the Ego incarnated, the creative centers are the lowest. In the Conqueror, who has become the Son of Astral Light, they are the highest.

This is the esoteric meaning of the Kabalistic maxim, "Demon est Deus inverses."

The generative function on the physical plane is strictly nothing but an animalistic one, and can never be anything else.

Obedience to the higher Law of Life demands its rigid control in man.

And while its lawful exercise for the continuation of the human race, in the semi-animal stage of its evolution, may not be considered harmful, its misuse, in any way, is fraught with the most terrible consequences both psychically and physically.

And the forces connected with it are used for abnormal purposes only in the foulest practices of sorcery, the inevitable result of which is rapid degeneration, declining health, and early death.

And that is the Lightning-Struck Tower.

STRENGTH.

THE DEVIL .

Chapter XIV

Card 8, GOOD (Strength) & Card 15, EVIL (Devil)

Card 8, Good

Card 8 is called Strength, Fortitude, and Justice by various commentators. The title given the card constrains the commentators to twist their interpretations of the symbol to fit the title of the card.

This charge may be laid against us, which matters not, for we shall formulate our interpretation of the card to fit the philosophy of the Ageless Wisdom preserved in the Bible.

The Ancient Cryptograms were based on the nature of Life and the constitution of Man. They were a cryptographic text-book of the Arcane Science that revolves round the philosophy of the Masters which begins in the second and third chapters of the first book of the Bible, as follows:

Of every Tree of the Garden thou mayest freely eat. But of the Tree of the Knowledge of Good and Evil, thou shalt not eat of it; for in the day thou eatest thereof, thou shalt surely die (Gen. 2:16, 17).

But the Voice of Temptation changed the thought of man:

In the day ye eat of the Fruit of the Tree in the midst of the Garden, then your eyes shall be opened, and ye shall be as gods, knowing Good and Evil (Gen. 3:3-5).

It is obvious that the subject here is Man. The Garden represents his body, in the Bible called the Temple of God. The care thereof was the great lesson of the Masters.

The allegory deals with that care of the body as to its sublimest function. The Tree symbolizes the sublimest part of the body. And man may freely use and enjoy all parts and processes of his body, *with one vital exception*.

Man is not only told these things but he is warned of the terrible consequences that will result automatically if he uses that one excepted function.

Here, thinly veiled, is presented the very core of the Major Arcana of the Masters. That is the philosophy symbolized by the Tarot.

The New Testament makes no direct reference to this philosophy, but the last book of the Bible does describe, in symbol and allegory, the effects experienced by the Neophyte in the ceremony of Initiation, in which he is taught the secret of achieving Seership by the conservation of the Solar Fire commonly consumed in animalistic generation.

The law of propagation is one of the strongest in nature, and rules everything with a rod of iron. So, in Card 8 this law is symbolized by the lion, the King of Beasts.

The picture of this card shows a woman closing the lion's mouth. In the earlier forms, the woman is opening the lion's mouth. The first alternative is better symbolically, but either is an instance of Strength in its conventional understanding, and conveys the idea of Mastery.

The unornamented white robe of the woman indicates purity. White is the color assigned to Kether, the Crown, which is the top circle on the Kabalistic diagram of the Tree of Life.

The woman represents Virgo, second sign of the earthly triad. The sign Leo (Lion) always precedes the ascension of Virgo. He prepares the way, and is mentioned in the Bible (Gen. 49:9, 10).

Over the woman's head hovers the same symbol of Life that appears in the card of the Magician, being the Lemniscate which represents the motion of the sidereal bodies and the astral character personified by the woman.

Eight was the occult number ascribed to Hermes, which is the digit value of the Four Elements and the Ineffable Name J H V H.

The lion, as the King of Beasts, represents in this case one of the strongest forces in Nature, generation.

Perception and chastity are the guiding principles of Virgo, and this sign exhibits the Ego externalized thru the Virgin or Pure Mind.

Virgo is associated with HE, the fifth Hebrew letter, which name and form are that of a window or place thru which comes the Light. It means to see; it signifies perception, the sense of Knowledge of Good and Evil.

In the Bible, Virgo is presented as a woman clothed with the sun, the moon under her feet, and on her head a crown of twelve stars (Rev. 12:1).

There she is portrayed as fleeing from the Great Red Dragon, symbol of carnal lust, while here she is closing the lion's mouth, indicating the subjugation of man's animalistic nature.

As the lower phase of mind is the shadow or reflected image, so to say, of the true mind, the lower phase of mind, symbolized as the lion having its mouth closed by Virgo, implies the Mastery of Sexuality.

The esoteric meaning of the symbolism of this card should now be understood. When we tame the lion, when we master the great urge of generation, we change the whole pattern of our life.

Card 15, Evil

To understand the esoteric message concealed in the symbolism of the Tarot, we must know the inner meaning of the Arcane Science, and the attributes assigned by the Masters to the solstitial signs of the Zodiakos.

In this card we are confronted with the signs Capricorn and Scorpio.

Capricorn is the tenth sign of the Zodiakos. The Hebrew Gedi, Kid, or Scapegoat was the symbol of Capricorn.

Many are the names which designated this sign. One of these was Seagoat, alluded to frequently by the ancients and seen in their Zodiakos and the pantheon of those distant days. The Egyptians designated it as the corcodile.

Esoterically considered, the sign indicated the darker mind emerging into the light, or the development of the higher aspects of the Ego on the terrestrial plane, where previously dwelt the dark, animalistic state.

Man then becomes the "anointed" one, before whom the Magi and wise men from the east laid their choicest presents (Mat. 2:1, 2).

For he who rises above the low level of animalism by subjugating the allurement of generation, is he who graduates in the conquest of his body; and supreme chastity was the most glorious crown that could be set before the Hierophants of the Temples.

Scorpio, Scorpion, also called the Eagle, is the eighth sign of the Zodiakos, and its ancient Hebrew name was Akrab, meaning conflict. Its chief star is Antares, which means wounding. This represents the Serpent in its enmity or opposition to the human Ego.

Scorpio is the sign that rules the sexual centers and signifies generation on the physical plane. Those born with this sign rising at birth, should above all seek to elevate the sexual desire.

When this has been accomplished, the deeper mystical sense is awakened, and instead of generation on the plane of animalism, the creative force is raised from the tail end to the head end, the plane of Seership.

The ancient myth of Scorpio's slaying Orion means the eradication of one aspect of mind that another may be developed and known.

Sexation imparts no lasting satisfaction to the higher phase of mind; and he who would become wise intellectually, must silently, slowly and surely break the shackles of this animalistic slavery.

There is no exception to cosmic law, and the king-like animals show a gradual abstinence in the use of the generative organs from the mouse to the moose.

And this is just as true of kingly man. The rajahic mind, which informs man of his own immortality, delights not in animalistic sensation.

When the solar force of the organism is not consumed in generation, it is gradually drawn back up to the brain, where it originates; and then and there will aid the Pituitary and Pineal glands in functional improvement.

The function of the Pineal is unknown to science; but the mystic is aware of its operation when in the inspired or ecstatic state. The joy of such moments is unknown to him who dwells only on the animalistic level.

- - - - - - -- - - -

We have briefly considered the qualities attributed by the Astrologers to the signs of Scorpio and Capricorn. Now we shall see how cleverly they wove these signs together to make their picture in Card 15.

In designing the picture of this card, the Astrologers relied upon the Zodiakos, indicating their belief that the signs implied the various aspects of the constitution and characteristics of Man.

They also indicated their belief in the doctrine, no doubt formulated by them, that those who partake of the "forbidden fruit" must pay the penalty without fail. For we do reap as we sow (Gen. 2:17; Gal. 6:7).

This card presents a Monster, termed the Devil by the Christian commentators, a word unknown to the Ancient Astrologers, and invented by the church by prefixing the letter "D" to the word Evil.

Cards 8 and 15 are companion cards, and their titles should be Good and Evil respectively.

The Church Fathers had possession of the Trumps Major, changed the word Good to God, and called card 8 Strength instead of Good. And then they prefixed the letter "D" to Evil, creating a Monster they called the Devil, thus giving their God an opponent.

According to the teachings of the church, this Devil developed into such a powerful opponent of the church God, that he has gained control of most of the Christian world, pushing its God back into a corner.

The Beast in card 15 has the head of a Goat, Capricorn. The legs and feet are those of Scorpio, the Eagle. The body is humanal, the right side being male and the left female, because what the Monster represents affects both man and woman.

A large, inverted Pentagram, shining with phosphorescent light, is on the forehead, indicating that man is ruled by his five senses which make him a prisoner in a physical body.

The Pentagram is the symbol of Man, appearing in Card 5, the Hierophant. The inverted Pentagram implies the reversal of the basic understanding of man's creative powers.

It is the erroneous knowledge of his creative qualities that helps to keep man in bondage and causes him to sink into degeneration.

The five senses are symbolized in various ways in the Bible. They are mentioned as "five loaves" in one place (Mat. 14:17). In another as "Five Kings" (Jos. 10:22-26).

Joshua smote the Five Kings and slew them, which means that he conquered the desires of his body and rose to the plane of Seership.

Just below the navel of the Beast appears the sign of Mercury. The right hand is upraised with fingers extended, being the reverse of that benediction which is given by the Hierophant in Card 5.

The Beast has the wings of a bat, indicating darkness, and on the palm of the right hand appears a symbol of Saturn, ruling in Capricorn, indicating intellectual darkness. In the left hand there is a flaming torch, inverted toward the earth, a symbol of sensuality and the dissipation of the Solar Fire.

The Beast is seated on a black pedestal. From an iron ring in the front of it, two chains extend to the necks of a man and a woman, standing before the Beast which towers above them on a high seat.

They are the same man and woman we saw in Card 6. But now they have horns, hoofs, and tails with fiery tips, implying the ruling power of their animalistic nature.

They were overcome by their five senses, and yielded to the "accursed" function of animalistic generation, "forbidden" in the second and third chapters of Genesis, and the precious Solar Fire of Creation is flowing out at the tail end of the body, when it should be conserved and caused to flow up to the head end, to improve the brain and promote mental function.

The strong angel of the Solar God, Mikael, who poured down the blessings of life upon the man and woman in Card 6, now goes into action. He appears to wage war against the Monster that has chained them in sexual slavery.

This battle is mentioned in the Bible as "war in heaven," where Mikael and his angels fought against the Dragon. And the Great Dragon, "that old serpent," was cast out into the earth, and the Monster's place was found no more in heaven (Rev. 12:7-9).

In this allegory, the Dragon is identical with the Monster in Card 15. He represents the principle of Desire in all its innumerable graduations, from the vaguest yearnings and the mere promptings of the appetites of the body, down to the grossest phases of passion and lust.

The "war in heaven" indicates the struggle in the mind to subjugate carnal lust, the curse of mankind.

Casting the Monster out into the earth signifies the victory of man over carnal lust, gained by the Neophyte under the teachings of the Masters,--that being one purpose of initiation (p. 49, Son of Perfection).

While the proper use of the sexual function for the propagation of the race, in the semi-animal stage, may not be considered harmful, its misuse, in any way, is fraught with the most terrible consequences both physically and psychically, and the forces connected with it are used for abnormal purposes only in the foulest practices of sorcery.

The insane asylums of the country are filled with the feeble-minded due to the consumption of the Solar Fire of the body in masturbation, fornication, and generation.

In the picture in Card 15, the loops of the chains around the necks of the victims are sufficiently large so they may lift them off their heads and regain their freedom if they desire.

This, together with the human intelligence appearing in their faces, indicates their bondage is temporary, depending on their own conduct. It is for them to determine whether the Beast who is exalted above them in the picture, shall be their master forever.

For the forces of the Macrocosm but await the time when the resurgent Divine Life again stirs within man, and then this child of the eons, whom the Scorpio-Capricorn Monster of Darkness can drag down till he is lower than the beasts, will again be exalted to his proper place in the Realm of Life.

The manifestation of the Creative Force in its aspect of sexuality, is the most potent factor in humanistic evolution, astral as well as physical. In fact, upon its rightful understanding and proper use rests the destiny of the race on this planet.

For only thru generation, and the lessons learned thru the manifestation of the Powerful Creative Force in its most dense and material aspect of Sexuality, can humanity achieve Regeneration.

This greatest of all Cosmic Forces, so far as Life is concerned, the Ancient Masters discovered how to control and to divert its powerful influence from Destruction to Construction.

The secret of their greatness was their discovery and application of the law which causes a shifting of the fever and makes this Creative Force work for man instead of against him.

This is the subject which constituted the leading theme covered by the ancient philosophy. It is treated in the Bible, in symbol and allegory, from

-118-

the first book to the last. It is the center of the Edenic parable and the parable and the point of Revelation.

The Great Red Dragon mentioned in Chapter 12 of Revelation symbolizes Carnal Lust, and the Seven Seals mentioned in Chapter 5 signifies the Seven Major Nerve Centers of the body which are dormantized by Carnal Lust.

The "tails with fiery tips" indicate that the Solar Fire of Life is dissipated on the animalistic plane in generation when its purpose in man, by conservation, is to exalt him to the angelistic plane.

We live in the Tail Age. The great majority of mankind has always lived in the Tail Age since the Division of the Sexes, which occurred millions of years ago.

The chief work of the Ancient Masters was devoted to lifting man up out of the Tail Age to his proper place on the angelistic plane, as shown by Hotema in his "Son of Perfection," and by Dr. George R. Clements in his startling work titled "The Virgin Birth" (in collaboration with Herbert M. Skelton.)

THE HERMIT.   TEMPERANCE.

Chapter XV

Card 9, The Hermit & Card 14, Time (Temperance)

Card 9, The Hermit

This may be considered as one of the more important of all the 22 cards of the Greater Arcana; and most commentators visualize it in the wrong light.

This card presents the picture of an old man who, in spite of his age and the further fact that as he walks he leans upon a Staff, he is strong, erect, alert, with bright eyes, looking directly ahead. He is clad in a long Mantle, and in his raised right hand he has a Lantern.

Most commentators think this symbolism represents the search for an honest man, or for Truth and Justice. A search for these would require a lighted lantern in broad daylight without doubt, but in this case this is a card of attainment, as we shall later see, rather than a card of quest.

Number 9 is primarily the Number of Initiation in the Ancient Mysteries.

And what was the purpose of Initiation? Not to teach the Neophyte to search for anything, but to teach him the mysteries of the Universe, of Life and of Man. It was to inform the man of darkness as to his own being and identity, and to explain to him his relationship to the Universe.

That was the very core, center and heart of all searching. So the 9th letter of the Hebrew alphabet is Teth, and is connected with the Zodiakol sign Leo, the core, center and heart of the Grand Man.

Another meaning of Teth is a Serpent, the most subtile of any beast of the field (Gen. 3:1). And as 9 is the Number of Initiation, so an Initiate was called a Naga, or Serpent of Wisdom.

The Bible says, "Be ye therefore wise as serpents" (Mat. 10:16).

. There is a further, important reason for the application of this term to the Initiate.

Just as the Serpent sheds and renews its outer skin, so the Initiate sheds his outer "Mantle of Darkness" and dons a new "Mantle of Light," which reveals that the process called "death" is not what it seems to be.

It is surprising to see that the biblical makers could not avoid including a hint of the ancient Doctrine of Reincarnation. They made Paul say, "In death, we shall not sleep, but we shall all be changed" (1 Cor. 15:51).

The Doctrine of Reincarnation formed the basis of the earliest of the ancient schools of philosophy. The Greek Philosopher Pherecydes taught it, and Pythagoras, Empedocles, Plato, Virgil and Ovid embraced it in their philosophies. It is found in Jewish literature, in the Talmud, in the writings of Philo, and is definitely proclaimed in the Kabalah.

Origen taught Life Universal and admitted Reincarnation. It was not until 553 A.D. that the Doctrine of Reincarnation of the Ancient Masters was banned by the Mother Church at the Second Council of Constantinople.

The Ancient Masters taught that the Ego goes thru Seven Incarnations. The Apocalyptic Allegory is woven around the Initiate who is in his sixth. He has gone thru five, and must go thru one more. That philosophy is contained in the Bible but stated in terms that can be understood only by an occultist. Here it is:

"And there are seven kings (reincarnations), (of whom) five have fallen, and one is, and the other has not yet come; and when he cometh, he must continue a short space" (Rev. 17:10).

In Greek philosophy the Ego was described as "more ancient than the body," because it had run the cycle of incarnations in many bodies, donning and doffing them as garments of contact with the terrenial world, and treasuring up the powers of all life generated in experience in every form of it.

The mutual relation of the Ego to the body in each of its incarnate periods is the nub of ancient philosophy, and the core of all biblical meaning.

The Egyptian "Book Of The Dead," said to be much older than any part of the Christian Bible, most majestically phrased the subject in these words: "The Ego, projecting itself into one physical embodiment after another, steppeth onward through eternity."

The ancient Hindu Master said: "Know thou, O Prince of Pandu, that there was never a time when I, nor thou, nor any of these princes of the earth, was not; nor will there ever come a time, hereafter, when any of us shall cease to be.

"As the Ego, wearing this material garment, experienceth the stages of infancy, youth, manhood, and old age, even so shall it, in due time, pass on to another body, and in other incarnations it shall again live, and move, and play its part.

"Those who have attained the wisdom of the Inner Doctrine, know these facts, and fail to be moved by aught that cometh to pass in this world of change — to such, Life and Death are but words, and both terms are but the surface aspects of the deeper being" (Bhagavad Gita, p. 25).

It should be observed that in the esoteric cosmogony, the theory of "dead" matter has no place. The universe is a manifestation of Life, of Consciousness, from the Sun down to the Electrons and Protons.

But in this philosophy, a sharp distinction is made between Being and Existence.

The Archetypal World is that of True Being, changeless, eternal. Existence is a going outward into the worlds of becoming, of ceaseless change and transformation.

The Ego, the Immortal Man, when incarnated, comes under the sway of this law of mutation, entering upon a long cycle of incarnations, passing from one mortal body to another.

For lack of space the metaphysical aspect of this subject will not be discussed; but it may be said that the fact of Reincarnation, so far from being mysterious and difficult of proof, is really very prosaic and simple, so that it has always been treated as exoteric in all archaic philosophies and religions.

Positive knowledge of its truth, on the basis of personal experience, was one of the first results obtained by him who entered upon the initial stages of self-conquest. It was then a fact as apparent to him as the cognate facts of birth and death.

Pythagoras believed above all things in Reincarnation. The traditions concerning his teachings indicate that he was an important champion of what used to be called the Doctrine of Metempsychosis, understood as the Ego's transmigration into successive bodies.

He himself had been (a) Ethalides, a son of Mercury; (b) Euphorbus, son of Panthus, who perished at the hands of Menelaus in the Trojan War; (c) Hermotimus, a prophet of Clazomenae, a city of Ionia; (d) an humble fisherman, and finally (e) the philosopher of Samos.

Those who desire to follow this phase of the subject further, should read "The Soul's Secret" by Hotema.

Ordinary views are based upon the assumption that the life of man rises

out of nothing
into nothing.

Christian
of the possib-
future life,
they do not
before birth.
the church,
born with

It is
think of
or of the inner
man, as a be-
cut of

and vanishes

teachings speak
ility of a
life, but
speak of life
According to
"souls" are
the bodies.

difficult to
life (soul)
being of
ing that rises
nothing.

It is   much easier to
think that this being already existed, before birth. But people are not taught
how to begin thinking in that direction. For such thinking would throw the
gospel Jesus out of a job.

The Ancient Masters taught that "death" is not the extinction and end of
man, as the masses believe, and as physical science teaches.

Death is that regular, orderly, lawful process of the Cosmic Cycle in
which the Ego is actually "born again" as stated in the Bible, but not correctly interpreted by priest and preacher (Jn. 3:3, 5, 7).

Hotema covered this in "Cosmic Creation" in which he shows that thru the
process called "death" the Ego sheds its material Mantle and returns to its
original home in the Astral World, to reappear in due time in the visible
world in the cosmic process called Reincarnation, or Recurrence, or Repetition, when the Ego will come again, clad in a new garment, made of the same
Four Elements.

According to theosophical authors, several hundred years, and very often
a thousand or even two thousand years, may elapse between one reincarnation
and another.

One purpose of Initiation was to teach the Neophyte this secret of Eternal Life. But the biblical makers changed all direct reference to Reincarnation and purposely muddied the waters to confuse the masses.

Number 9 also completes and discards the old digits, which might be compared to the discardation of the Serpent's skin, and emerges in the new number
10. Digits 10, 20, 30, etc., are the same as the first, but with the power
of 10 added to each.

The letter Teth is also connected with astral electricity, which the
Masters discovered ages ago. They represented it by the Serpent, for Fohat
hisses as he glides hither and thither, in zigzags, as electricity does.

The Kabalah figures it with the letter Teth, whose symbol is the Serpent
which played a prominent part in the Ancient Mysteries, and from which it

was adopted by the biblical makers. Its cosmic number is 9, for it is the ninth letter of the alphabet and also the ninth Gate.

The Number 9 is the Magic Agent par excellence, and designated in Hermic philosophy as "Life infused into Primordial Matter, the essence that compos s all things, and the Ego that determines their form." .

Scientists have now discovered that everything in the universe basically consists of electricity, a fact known to the Masters hundreds of thousands of years ago, and disclosed by a correct interpretation of their symbols.

The Masters regarded Astral Electricity, also called Astral Light, as the Initiator of Matter.

The age of the Hermit in this picture does not denote senility, but the vigor of maturity, hence experience, discretion and wisdom.

Most Cartomancers consider the Hermit with his Lantern as a wise man in search of Truth which is located far off in the sequence, and of Justice which has preceded him on the way. Others regard him as the Capuchin, and in more philosophical language, the Sage.

As stated above, this card is a symbol of attainment rather than that of quest.

The lighted Lantern the Hermit holds above his head symbolizes the Star of Wisdom.

The Mantle which envelops him and partially hides the lighted Lamp, is the Robe of Discretion with which the Initiate must enwrap himself from the gaze of the multitude and shield the full flare of his Lamp of Wisdom from the eyes of the world.

The Staff upon which he leans is the Magic Wand, the Caduceus, the symbol of the Creative Principle, Aaron's Rod of Power, which budded, the Seven Buds representing the unfolded Seven Sense Powers of the Seer.

Some commentators regard the Hermit as symbolizing the doctrine of occult isolation as a protection of personal magnetism against admixture.

This is one of the frivolous renderings of Eliphas Levi, which considers the Hermit as the Silent and Unknown Philosopher enveloped in his Mantle to conceal his knowledge from the profane.

The Lantern of the Hermit is the Light of Wisdom that reveals the dark, dangerous gullies in the Path of Life, into which the masses fall to their ruin, along with the blind leaders of the blind (Mat. 15:14).

That Light is the blazing Six Pointed Star, which indicates to the occultist who can read the Hieroglyphic language, that the Hermit is an Initiate of the

Ancient Mysteries who possesses the esoteric knowledge that the Microcosm is a miniature reflection of the Macrocosm.

The Seal of Solomon was a hexagonal figure consisting of two interlaced triangles, forming the outlines of a six-pointed Star. It came to be called the Eastern Star and the Star of Bethlehem.

The White Triangle points up, symbolical of the Astral World. The Black triangle points down, symbolical of the Physical World. This was the symbol of the unition of the Celestial and Terrestrial Worlds, which is Creation.

The Zodiakos is a Circle enclosing the Six-pointed Star. The lower half, of the circle symbolizes the Terrestrial World. The Cross within the circle is the Cross of Life, on which man hangs in the Terrestrial World for "evil purposes," using his body to satisfy lusts for sensation, greed, hate, jealousy, etc.

When Roman Catholicism had crushed the Ancient Mystery schools, it took over the ancient Cross of Life, hung its Jesus on it, then proclaimed that this resulted in taking away the sins of the world (Jn. 1:29).

Number 9 is the Astral Reflection which reveals cosmic secrets in all their abstract power, and banishes superstition rising from the unknowable, and the silly urge to worship Totem Poles and Crucified Saviors.

The Masters made 9 the Number of Initiation, because the Initiate reigns over superstition and darkness, and by Wisdom alone can man advance thru the mysteries of Life, leaning upon his Staff, enveloped in his Mantle, and lighted by his Lamp of Wisdom.

When the newly born Ego appears in the visible world, clad in the Mantle of Nature, surrounded by intellectual darkness as to his origin and destiny, and besieged on all sides by enemies that prey upon the ignorant, the uninformed Mind is easily misled and impressed by a continuous series of illusions in the visible world, which are considered as real by the profane, the man of darkness.

In that state, Man becomes deceived and lost in the fog of illusion, due to ignorance of the Law of Mutation.

Born into a world of constantly changing things and forms, being in darkness as to his own true nature, man believes that he is the product of these unstable things, regards himself as a separate existence, falls an easy victim of the schemers and tricksters, and embraces all sorts of superstition and idolatry.

It is easily understood why man needs the True Light of Wisdom. For that purpose were founded the Ancient Mysteries, in which select persons were taught that man is the center of all worlds, united to all things, and the Visible Cosmos is the material Mantle which clothes his Ego, the Eternal Entity which existed before the creation of the earth, is independent of the body, and continues its existence after the material Mantle returns to dust, all of which Hotema explains in "Cosmic Creation."

So, the Fool of Card 0 becomes, by Initiation, the Wise Man of Card 9, and the state of Hermitage symbolizes the Life the Wise Man must lead because he is out of step with the socialized pattern, is distrusted by his associates, and hated by all institutions that live on darkness and thrive on ignorance.

Card 14, Time

The fact that this card has been called Temperance offers an obvious instance of a meaning behind a meaning, which is the title in chief to consider in respect to the Tarot as a whole.

This Arcanum is called Temperance fantastically, because, when the rule of it obtains in our consciousness, it tempers, combines, and harmonizes the astral and physical natures. Under that impression we know in our rational part something of whence we came and whither we are bound.

The principal features of the symbolism of this card are designed to appraise the Neophyte that for him the element called Time is non-existent.

The angel is Michael, one of the four angels of the Solar God. He is the merciful, the patient, the holy, with the sign of the Sun on his head, and on his breast the square and triangle of the septenary.

In his hands he holds two cups, one of silver and one of gold. Between them there incessantly flows a stream that sparkles with all the colors of the rainbow. It cannot be determined from which cup it flows and into which it is flowing.

One cup represents the past, the other the future. The stream between them is the present.

This symbolizes Time in its most incomprehensible aspect for the man of darkness, who is taught to believe that everything flows in one direction. He sees not that everything constantly meets, that one thing comes from the past and another from the future, and that Time is just a multitude of Circles, turning in different directions.

The interpretation of this symbolism discloses that Time is not what the man of darkness thinks it is. Time is just another illusion of the five senses.

Everything is. There is one eternal present, the Eternal Now. Time is only a condition of the perception of the world by our five senses.

Separate Time is a completed circle.

We can think of Time as a straight line only on the straight line of the Great Time. But the Great Time does not exist, so every separate Time can be only a circle.

The Light in the Hermit's Lantern is the blazing Six-pointed Star, which represented the World in Ancient Symbolism. In reality, it is the symbolism of Space-Time, or the "period of dimensions," i.e., of the three Space Dimensions and the three Time Dimensions in their perfect union, where every point of Space includes the whole of Time, and every moment of Time includes the whole of Space, when everything is everywhere and always.

The laws of Time and Eternity are illogical. They cannot be studied within the four rules of mathematics. To understand them, we must be able to think irrationally and without "facts."

Nothing is more deceptive than "facts" when all the facts that refer to the question under consideration are not available, and we must deal with accessible facts which distort our vision and lead us astray.

When we have no general plan of Creation and Creative Processes, we can not know whether we have a sufficient quantity of facts for judgment in this or that direction.

Modern science has no general plan of Creation and Creative Processes, and that is the reason why we have no science now. The so-called scientific systems are based on many assumptions and "some facts," and these systems are as deficient as the facts on which they are based.

Modern science is an illusion. It confines its work to superficial descriptions, and not to the elucidation of fundamental causes. It loudly heralds its descriptive discoveries and silently hides its explanatory failures.

Science cannot explain the simplest of creative processes. It is nothing more than learned ignorance. It uses rhetorical devices to conceal immense areas of the unknown that it calls science.

Science has in its backyard a large rubbish dump of discarded and exploded theories that once formed part of its alleged infallible foundation.

If you question any of the accepted theories of science, you are apt to be called a heretic, and receive the sneers, smears, and innuendoes of the unthinking mob that accepts those prevailing theories.

And if you dare question what has been established as "science", you may even be denied freedom of speech and of the press. In fact, that has been taking place for years. In the last decade some four hundred people have been barred from the mail for attacking these "established facts" of science.

In order to reach the laws of Time and Eternity, we must start with knowledge of that state in which no Time and Eternity oppose each other. For if Time and Eternity have a beginning, we must consider that point before that beginning began.

The Eternal Now is the state in which "everything is everywhere and always," that is, in which every point of Space touches every point of Time, and which is the state expressed in the ancient symbolism by the intersecting triangles, a Six Pointed Star.

The Blazing Six Pointed Star in the Hermit's Lantern is to signify that he has discovered the Eternal Now.

In the 10th Chapter of Revelation appears an allegory directly related to the Hermit, to seership, and to Time. We shall paraphrase:

-127-

I saw another mighty Divinity come down from the sky, clad with a cloud, a rainbow upon his head, his face luminous like the sun, and his feet like pillars of fire.

He held a little scroll unrolled. Placing his right foot upon the sea and his left upon the earth, he cried out with a loud voice, and seven thunders uttered their voices.

I was about to record the teachings of the seven thunders, but heard a voice from the sky saying to me:

"Seal up (the teachings) which the seven thunders uttered, and record them not." .

(The voices of the seven thunders were mystery-teachings, not intended for the exoteric and the profane).

And the Divinity lifted up his hand to the sky, and swore by the Macrocosmic Ego who lives forever and ever, who brought into existence the sky and what is in it, the earth and what is in it, and the sea and what is in it, that Time shall be no more.

But in the days of the voice of the seventh Divinity, when he shall begin to sound, also shall be made perfect the Mystery of the Ego (Rev. 10: 1-7).

The Voice of the Seventh Divinity begins to sound when man has developed his seven principles and his seven powers. Then the Mystery of the Ego is revealed.

In the ritual of initiation in the Ancient Mysteries, when the neophyte had mastered the seven principles and the seven powers, thus activating the "third eye" (Pineal gland of the brain), he became a Seer and passed beyond the illusion of Time.

It is only a crude, unphilosophical notion of the man of darkness that Eternity is "a long period of time."

Time is neither an entity nor a thing per se. Nor is Eternity merely Time indefinitely prolonged.

Time is a mental concept rising from the consciousness of change in the phenomenal world; whereas Eternity is noumenal, changeless, extending neither into the "past" nor the "future". It is an immeasurable "present".

To the human Ego there is no Time. Only change. Time affects the material Mantle in which the Ego is clad on the material plane.

This phase of the subject is discussed more fully under Card 20, Reincarnation.

THE SEVEN THUNDERS

The fable of the Seven Thunders was alluded to in Card 17, the Star. It relates to the Mind, the most colossal power in the world, and yet so seriously limited by the Five Senses that it is able to contact only a small part of the Universe.

When the Mind breaks thru the narrow limitation imposed by the Five Senses, man's Consciousness is liberated and contacts a vastly expanded world, of which dreams and visions are manifestations.

This is the esoteric interpretation of the biblical fable concerning Joshua and the Five Kings (five senses), which he slew, cast into a cave, and put great stones at the cave's mouth to prevent their possible escape (Jos. 10: 5-16).

The science of the biblical Joseph, who accomplished remarkable things in Egypt, was none other than a comprehension of the natural analogies which subsist between ideas and images, or between the Word J H V H and its symbols.

Joseph knew that the Ego, when released from the restricted imposition of the Five Senses and immersed by sleep in the Astral Light, perceives the reflections of its most secret thoughts and even of its presentiments. He knew further that the art of translating the hieroglyphics of sleep is the Key of Universal lucidity, seeing that all intelligent beings have revelations in dreams.

In sleep, the Five Senses are dormant, inactive, and the Mind is then free to roam the Universe at will. This knowledge inspired the Ancient Masters to search for ways and means to free the Mind, while awake, from the limitations imposed by the Five Senses.

Their discoveries were guarded with great care because the knowledge was so startling. It was imparted only to the Neophyte in the ceremony of initiation, as described by Hotema in "Son of Perfection."

The Masters discovered that the sixth sense (Pituitary gland in the brain) is both a receiving and transmitting instrument, and that the seventh sense organ (Pineal) functions in conjunction with the sixth. When it functions under control of the Ego in the waking state, a phenomenon occurs that is amazing to those who are present.

Of course, the seventh sense must function to a limited degree at all times, or there would be no manifestation of life in the physical body, as explained by Hotema in "The Flame Divine." (The Breath of Life and The Flame Divine).

But it is rare that man progresses in physical development, in knowledge and understanding, sufficiently to realize the full range of the seventh sense -- how to direct its functions and how to exercise free will in its uses.

The Masters who knew how to use and direct the seventh sense, possessed powers which would appear supernatural to the average man. So, those who have discovered how to use and direct the use of this sense with a marked degree of understanding, have gone down in legend and history as gods and supermen.

The secret society of the Magi is no doubt the oldest organization in the world, and extends back into the night of time. They teach no one who has not been prepared, tested, and accepted, and they record their esoteric knowledge only in symbols to represent sounds and convey thought forms.

The written records contained in the hieroglyphics engraved in stone and on metal plates of the long dead past, tell of civilizations that reached heights which, in some respects, far exceeded our own; and they left us a picture of what we may expect as we rise to the apex of our own civilization.

These records describe a civilization that perished with the sinking of Lemuria and Atlantis, as related by Hotema in "Cosmic Creation." They show that man has been on this earth for millions of years.

WHEEL of FORTUNE.

DEATH.

Chapter XVI

Card 10, Wheel of Life & Card 13, Wheel of Death

Card 10, WHEEL OF LIFE

For countless ages man gazed into the sky and saw the stars always kept their relative positions, but that the entire sky revolved around its axis every night in slow, majestic grandeur.

It is a whirling universe, said they. And science says our Solar System developed from Whirling Chaos.

That is the Law Of The Cosmic Cycle.

Discovering the Law Of The Cosmic Cycle, the Ancient Astrologers, after ages of study and research, divided the orbital path of the planets into twelve divisions, making the Earth's course, or apparently the Sun's course thru them for twelve solar months, one year.

Our solar system lies in a plane, somewhat in the form of a fried egg. We see the whole system moving in what appears to be a narrow path in the sky.

The Sun, the Earth, the planets and the moon seem to move in a narrow strip of the sky, and this strip the ancients called the Taeodeem.

How it came to be called the Zodiakos is not clear; but it is generally believed to be of Greek origin, derived from the Greek word for little animals, zodion, a diminutive form of zoon, "an animal." And so, it was called the animal circle, and is mentioned in the Bible (Ezek. 1: 13-19).

Taeod is a Hebrew word for step, and Akos (Echo) is the Greek verb "to have." The signification of the two words, taken together, is "having steps," -- steps of the Sun in his apparent daily and yearly march thru the sky.

It has now been realized that the signs of the Zodiakos are not of Greek origin at all. They are far older than the oldest Greek civilization, and go back into the darkness of antiquity.

It was the work of the Roman Catholic Church in re-shaping ancient history that gave Greece the credit for most all ancient knowledge.

Even the etymology has been disputed. Some claim the word is not Greek at all, but comes from a pre-Semitic root which stands for a walk, or a way -- referring to the zodiakol signs as "steps" in a way around the sky.

The zodiakol signs were differently named in different countries, and it seems we owe our present system of dividing the heavens to the early Chaldeans.

The whole schemata was for the purpose of demonstrating the relation existing between the Macrocosm and the Microcosm.

Physical man is the image of the Grand Archetypal Man seen in the heavens above, and the twelve signs of the Zodiakos correspond to the Human Temple, which is acted upon by thought, motion and vibration.

As we dig back into the prehistoric past, we discover that the ancient hieroglyphics of the Zodiakos mean far more than we at first are inclined to believe, thanks to the teaching of the church.

The facts and principles of life were much better understood then than they are now, and cosmic evolution was portrayed in these symbols.

And while we may reasonably believe that much romance, sentiment and fiction entered into their symbolism, yet we are struck with wonder again and again at the successful manner in which they grappled with the more recondite problems of biology, psychology and physiology.

When we search deeply into the meanings of their ideographs, we discover that the myths of the Zodiakos referred to the mysteries of the Human Ego.

Coulson Turnbull said: "The twelve allegorical labors of the god and savior Hercules, represented the passage of the Sun thru the twelve different signs of the Zodiakos" (The Divine Language of Celestial Correspondence).

A. B. Kingsford wrote: "The Soul's (Ego's) history is written in the stars" (The Perfect Way).

Marcion, the author of the Mark Gospel of the New Testament, said that the gospel Jesus simply represents the passage of the Sun thru the twelve different signs of the Zodiakos, and his 12 disciples represent these 12 signs.

In referring to the Pauline Epistles, he said: "The principal foundation of those epistles was the sign of the Zodiakos, known as Aries, the Ram or Lamb" (Antiquity Unveiled).

The numbers and letters of the Hebrews which related entirely to the principles and conditions of the Human Ego, were first traced out like the constellations.

Their first twelve letters and numbers correspond to the 12 zodiakol constellations, commencing with Taurus and ending with Aries; and the rest of their 22 letters are also an astral alphabet.

The Zodiakos, then, represents the Macrocosm, and man's physical body corresponds to it.

Man's body is composed on the physical plane to receive and respond to the impressions from the unit whole. The mystery of Life will baffle the intellect until this is realized.

The Macrocosm and the Microcosm operate and correspond to a uniform mathematical law whether from plant or planet, angle-worm or angel, from the vegetation which carpets the Earth to the stars which gem the sky.

The great lesson man must learn is to intellectualize sensible products to their occult analogy. Man will then begin to discover everywhere the One Law of the Macrocosm.

This fact is now coming to be observed in the researches of modern physics. Man is an infinitely compounded unit, a living mirror of the universe. The Zodiakos is our clock of destiny.

Out of this work of the Ancient Astrologers, the Zodiakos became the Wheel of Life, and out of the Wheel of Life logically emerged the Tarot, also the Wheel of Life; and it was used by the Ancient Masters to teach the man of darkness the nature of Life and the constitution of Man.

And that is the origin and the source of the only science the world has ever had that deals intelligently and systematically with Anthropology, Biology, Psychology, Physiology and Pathology.

Then, in the 4th century A.D., came the birth of the Roman Catholic Church, and that ended the Light of the World.

As the success of the Church depended upon darkness and ignorance, a vigorous, brutal and bloody campaign was conducted for three hundred years to crush and obliterate the only Science of Man the world has ever had.

This wanton work of torture, blood and destruction was so well prosecuted, that in the middle of the 5th century, Archbishop Chrysostom boasted:

"Every trace of the old philosophy and literature of the ancient world has vanished from the face of the earth" (Doane, Bible Myths, P. 436).

The result of this destruction has been that even today the Christian world is in darkness as to the nature of Life and the constitution of Man.

That great doctor, Alexis Carrel, wrote: "Man is made up of a procession of phantoms, in the midst of which there strides an unknowable reality" (Man The Unknown, p. 4).

And Dr. Robert A. Millikan, world renowned scientist, head of the California Institute of Technology, authority on Cosmic Rays, said:

"I cannot explain why I am alive rather than dead. Physiologists can tell me much about the mechanical and chemical processes of my body, but they cannot say why I am alive" (Collier's, Oct. 24, 1925).

Wisdom is meaningless unless it leads to the solution of the mystery of Life. We cannot properly evaluate our relationships with the visible and invisible worlds until we discover the nature of Life and the constitution of Man.

And that summarizes the sad condition of the Christian world in the realm of science so far as Life and Man are concerned.

Very different from the wild propaganda of the controlled press and big periodicals as to what science knows about Life and Man.

And so, we are forced to go back to the Ancient Astrologers, those "superstitious heathens" according to the Church, and let them guide us thru the darkness and wilderness in this field where modern knowledge is so woefully wanting.

Card 10 is called the Wheel of Life and also the Wheel of Fortune, but those who designed the Tarot were interested in man, not in money.

For good reasons the biblical makers were careful to see the Bible contained no direct reference either to the Zodiakos or the Tarot. They did include a brief account of Ezekiel's vision of "wheels" and "living creatures" which meant the Zodiakos and its signs (Ezek. 1: 14-19).

They also adopted from Tarot Card 20 the Doctrine of the Resurrection. Then the Christian commentators on the Tarot, either because of ignorance or to mislead the masses, changed the title to "The Last Judgment."

And they then applied the Doctrine of the Resurrection literally to their mythical Jesus, carefully excluding all the rest of humanity, except those who believe in this Jesus (Jn. 3: 16).

The word "Tarot" itself means a wheel or something that rotates. Human language was made of this Wheel. Thus, ORB-IT means "the going of the Orb," and even the rut in the road made by the wheel is called "Orbita," because the rut shows the route or road of the Wheel.

In the opinion of the Ancient Astrologers, the Life Element was a substantial movement, or a substance which eternally and essentially moved.

This substance is indefectible, incorruptible, and immortal. But its manifestations in the world of form are subject to eternal mutation by the perpetuity of movement.

Thus, all dies because all lives.

Were it possible to make eternal any formation of matter, motion would then be arrested, and thus would be created the only real death. So, the Wheel of Life must constantly rotate.

To imprison the Ego forever in a mummified human body, would be the terrible solution of that magical paradox concerning pretended immortality in the same body and on the same earth.

That condition was foreign to the mind of those ancient men who said, "He will swallow up death in victory" (Is. 25: 8); and "the last enemy that shall be destroyed is death" (1 Cor. 15: 26).

Death is not an enemy to be destroyed. It is not the termination of Life. It is a natural change, a cosmic process as natural as that of changing ice to invisible vapor; as natural as the condition called "birth." It refers only to appearance, to observation, to what we see, and not to what actually occurs.

All is regenerated by the universal dissolvent of the primal substance. The force of this dissolvent is concentrated in the quintessence -- that is to say, at the equilibrating center of a dual polarity.

The Four Elements of the Arcane Science which we have often mentioned, and which are symbolized in the Sphinx, are the Four Forces of the Universal Magnet, represented by the figure of the Solar Cross, the Cross of Life, which revolves indefinitely around its own center, and so propounds the enigma respecting the quadrature of the Circle.

The magnetic state of polarization of the astral bodies results from their equilibrated gravitation around the cosmic suns, which are the common reservoir of the electro-magnetism.

The vibration of the quintessence around the common reservoir manifests as Astral Light, the polarization of which is revealed by colors.

White (colorless) is the color of the quintessence. This color condenses toward its negative pole as blue, and becomes fixed as black; while it condenses toward its positive pole as yellow, and becomes fixed as red.

Thus centrifugal life force proceeds from black to red, passing by the white; and centripedal life force returns from red to black, following the same order.

The four intermediate or mixed hues produce, with the primary colors, what are called the seven colors of the prism and the solar spectrum.

These seven colors form the seven atmospheres or seven luminous zones round each sun, and the planet which is dominant in each zone is magnetized in a manner analogous to the color of its atmosphere, according to the science of Astrology.

All creation is preserved by equilibrium and renewed by activity. Equilibrium in order and activity signifies progress.

The science of equilibrium and movement was the Arcane Science of the Ancient Astrologers. It is constituted in harmony with the number seven -- the septenary being expressed as the number of the Creative Week.

The Key to the Arcane Science is established on the number 4 -- which is that of the enigmatic forms of the Sphinx and of elementary manifestations. The Sphinx represents the equilibrium.

Dr. Waite said: "Sometimes the Sphinx is represented couchant on a pedestal above in Card 10, which defrauds the symbolism by stultifying the essential idea of stability amidst movement."

Concerning the Wheel of Life, Ouspensky wrote:

"And I heard the voice of the animals of Zarathustra:

" 'Everything goes, everything returns; eternally rolls the wheel of being.

" 'Everything dies, everything blossoms forth again; eternally runs the year of being.

" 'Everything breaks, everything is united anew; eternally builds itself the same house of being.

" 'Everything parts, everything meets again; the ring of being remains eternally true to itself.

" 'Being begins in every Now, around every Here rolls the sphere of There. The middle is everywhere. Circular is the Path of Eternity.' "

The Zodiakos is the Wheel of Life. It is a complicated symbol that was formulated by the Ancient Astrologers after ages of research and discovery disclosed man's relation to the Universe.

The Zodiakos is a chart that represents the perpetual motion of the fluidic universe and the flux of human life.

This Wheel is not pictured the same in the various Tarot cards. But in ancient symbology it was pivoted upon the top end of a staff, while at the base are two entwined serpents, signifying the dual properties of Polarity, as in the case of the Caduceus.

Poised with extended wings above the top of the Wheel was the Sphinx, representing the Four Elements of Creation and the quaternary constitution of Man.

The figure had paws of a lion, and in its right paw it held a sword, symbol of power or authority; and it was crowned with the symbol of Venus.

On the right side of the Wheel appeared Hermanubis (Hermes-Anubis), the jackal-headed god, symbol of Good, ascending, bearing in his right hand the Magic Wand (Caduceus), and having on his head the symbol of Mercury.

On the left side of the Wheel appeared Typhon (Set), the Egyptian god of Evil, descending with a trident in his hand.

These two figures on the Wheel of Life indicate that Good is ever aspiring and ascending, while Evil is ever descending into darkness and disintegrating.

Anubis and Typhon, representing Good and Evil, indicate that Evil must descend and be disintegrated so that its force may be liberated and manifest as Good at the next upward turn of the Wheel.

In his work titled "The Soul's Secret", Hotema referred to Tarot Card 10, Wheel of Life, and said:

"The Astrologers taught what physical science has recently discovered, that all things in the universe travel in circles, making the end and the beginning one and the same. For instance, the sun sets as it rises, and rises as it sets.

"The Astrologers applied this cosmic law to Life and Man, and declared that man dies in the astral world as he is born in the physical world, and dies in the physical world as he is born in the astral world.

"That is The Soul's Secret, and that is the substance of the Inner Doctrine that was symbolized in the Wheel of Life.

"So, according to the Wheel of Life, man is bound and ruled by a ceaseless circle of births and deaths, -- the Law of Reincarnation taught in all the ancient religions and philosophies, and condemned by the Church because it eliminates the service of its Jesus as the Savior of Souls."

"There is no observable action in the entire universe which is not FUNDA-MENTALLY dependent for its continuity upon CYCLIC CHANGE, -- and as surely as day follows night, so MUST LIFE FOLLOW DEATH" (Eternal Time, By Dr. James Clark.)

IMMORTALISM

"If a man die, shall he live again" (Job 14:14) is a burning question that rises with the dawn of the race.

Literature that has lasted the longest is that which has been based upon a desire for or an expectation or actual knowledge of, a future life.

"There is no death," wrote Huntley, in "Harmonics of Evolution," and added, "Life after physical death is a fact scientifically demonstrable."

Now, according to Christian dogma, Life is ruled by belief, not by law. Its religious system rests upon the following unscientific statement:

"For God so loved the world that he gave his only begotten Son, that whosoever believeth in Him should not perish, but have everlasting life" (Jn. 3: 16).

There are many reasons why this statement should not be taken seriously.

First, there are at least three different Gods mentioned in the Bible, and we are not told which of these Gods gave the world "His only begotten Son."

Second, this arbitrary, unnatural dogma fails to fit in a Universe of law and order, in which every cosmic phenomena and process occur according to immutable law.

These reasons are sufficient to show that it is useless to give any attention to this dogma, so we shall pass it by and put Life under the law and consider it scientifically.

Dr. Robert Walter made this shrewd observation: "The immortality of Life is proved in the same way as the indestructibility of matter. ...

"The human being surely becomes individualized once for all, and having learned much from earthly experience, he returns (in death to the the astral realm) from whence he came, to carry with him thru all the future whatever he may have gained (on earth).

"It is not to be presumed that man's experiences for gain will ever cease, and he necessarily takes with him the products of the past. ...

"When dynamite explodes, the force is not lost, but has changed its position.

"Just so with man when he dies. He has not lost his life, but has changed his position, going forward to another state" (Vital Science).

The process called "death" is not understood, nor is it generally known that cosmic phenomena move in cycles, as vapor to water to ice, and from ice back to water and to vapor.

Nothing is lost; nothing but form begins, and nothing but form ends.

Many ask, "Why are we here?" To that question Dr. James Clark gives a scientific answer in his "Eternal Time," in this striking observation:

"The only justification for (man's) existence is gain. Existence of a Life Form, via a physical body, results in the gain of action (on the earth plane). Existence in the death phase, without any form of body, results in the gain of no action (on the visible plane).

"The life and death phases (of the Ego) are coexisting essentials in continuing (man's) existence; and the existence of either (phase) without the presence of the other (phase) is an impossibility.

"The realization (of the cosmic cycle) in full understanding that no state (of existence) can ever begin unless some other previous state is ending, enables us at last to see with clear vision that man may spend a lifetime in action as a Life Form, studying in any one of the many "Temples", and no matter the lofty architecture, nor the awe-inspiring design of the High Altar as seen in St. Peter's, Rome, or the Cyclotron in Harwell, England, there is only one incident of major and fundamental importance that can ever happen to him.

"And this incident provides all the reason there can ever be for having

-138-

lived -- which is the insuring of the Cycle in the Eternal Action of Life, and
thus creating with certainty the supreme privilege and reward of living again
-- HE CAN DIE! (Without death, there could be no future life -- Hotema).

"There is no observable action in the entire Universe that is not funda-
mentally dependent for its continuity upon Cyclic Change; and as surely as day
follows night, so MUST LIFE AGAIN FOLLOW DEATH."

That scientific philosophy meets the test of law, is hoary with age, and
was taught by all the Ancient Masters for thousands of years before Christianity was ever invented. It appears in the Bhagavad Gita as follows:

"Know thou, O Prince of Pandu, that there never was a time when I, nor
thou, nor any of these princes of the earth, was not; nor shall there ever
come a time hereafter when any of us shall cease to be. (The Ego is as eternal as the stars. -- Hotema).

"As the Ego, wearing this material form, experienceth the stages of infancy, youth, manhood and old age, even so shall it, in due time, pass on to
another body, and in subsequent incarnations shall it again live (on the earth
plane), and move, and play its part.

"Those (wise ones) who have attained the wisdom of the Inner Doctrine,
know these secrets, and fail to be moved by aught that cometh to pass in this
world of change. To such, Life and Death are but words (of description), and
both (words) are but the surface aspects of the deeper being."

In that very ancient scroll, the Egyptian Book of the Dead, it is stated
that the Ego, "projecting itself into one physical embodiment after another,
'steppeth onward thru eternity' " (Kuhn, in Lost Light, p. 41).

This ancient philosophy appears in the Christian Bible, but is not understood by the masses because not correctly presented by the preacher, who may not
understand it himself. And if it were correctly and clearly presented, that
preacher would not only be unfrocked, but that knowledge would bring the end of
orthodox Christianity and dispose of its Jesus.

The Bible definitely says: "Behold, I show you a mystery: We shall not
sleep (in death), but we shall be changed" (to Immortality). -- 1 Cor. 15: 51.

And so, according to cosmic law, ancient philosophy and the findings of
modern science, when man dies he simply changes to another state, just as the
Bible says.

The only "mystery" surrounding the cosmic process called death, rises
from ignorance and false teaching.

And here again Dr. Clark points out the fact, that there is only one incident of major and fundamental importance that can ever happen to man, -- and
that indicates how exceedingly futile it is for man "to spend a lifetime in
action as a Life Form, studying in any of the Temples" anywhere on earth, under
the foolish, silly impression that he will learn from the teachers some mysterious secret of Life.

Dr. Clark said: "All the mystery surrounding Life is dependent upon the continuous creation of the Unknown."

Card 13, WHEEL OF DEATH

What is commonly called Life and Death are two aspects of the same Wheel.

The Wheel of Life brings the Ego into the physical world, and the Wheel of Death takes the Ego back to its original home in the Astral World.

In some cases this card presents a crude notion of the Reaping Skeleton, in others, a horseman on a white charger, clad in black armour, with a black helmet, and a black plume.

The Skeleton's face looks out from under the helmet. One bony hand holds a black banner, and the other holds black reins, ornamented with skull and cross-bones.

The black banner is emblazoned with the Mystic Rose held in the left hand of the Fool, which signifies Life.

Between two pillars on the verge of the horizon there shines the setting Sun of Immortality. The card with the Reaping Skeleton shows a river behind him, flowing toward the Sun.

Ouspensky said:

"Looking at the disappearing horseman and the setting Sun, I understood the Path of Life to consist of the hoofmarks of the Steed of Death.

"The Sun, setting on the one side, rises on the other. Every moment of its motion is a setting at one point and a rising at another.

"And I understood that, just as the Sun rises in its setting and sets in its rising, so Life sets in the astral realm as it rises in the physical realm, and rises again in the astral realm as it sets in the physical realm (Jn. 3:3, 5, 7).

" 'Yes,' said the Voice, 'You think the Sun has only one aim, to rise and set. These are only appearances. The Sun goes on its way, over its own orbit, round its gravitational center, and its risings and settings are mere illusions.

" 'Life and Death, Sunrise and Sunset -- are you not aware that all these appearances are but thoughts, illusions, dreams and fears of the Fool?' "

LAW OF MUTATION

True Being, the Ego, is changeless and eternal. Physical existence is birth from the World of Being into the World of Becoming (visible).

The Ego, when incarnated on the terrestrial stage of change, is ruled by the Law of Mutation, entering upon a long cycle of incarnations.

The Ancient Masters taught that the Ego goes thru seven incarnations, and this is mentioned in the last book of the Bible, as follows:

"And there are seven kings (incarnations),(of which) five are fallen, and one is, and the other is not yet come; and when he cometh, he must continue a short space." (Rev. 17: 10).

The Apocalypse describes, in symbol and allegory, the initiation of the Neophyte in the Ancient Mysteries, and the Neophyte, in this case, was in his sixth incarnation, as explained by Hotema in "Son of Perfection."

When the Ego, clad in its physical garment, appears in the physical world, surrounded by many dangers and mysteries, the mind of the man of darkness is impressed by one continuous series of illusions, which he considers real. His teachers, as well as he, are lost in the fog of illusion because they are not taught the Cycle of Life.

At this point Man needs Light. This need led to the founding of the Ancient Mysteries, in which the Neophyte was taught the secrets of Life.

The Ancient Astrologers did not follow the rule of modern science. They did not reason from observation, from the things which are seen. They had discovered how deceptive man's five faulty senses are, and based their conclusions on the things which are not seen. They said:

"The things which are seen (with the eyes) are temporal; but the things which are not seen (with the eyes) are eternal" (2 Cor. 4: 18).

They concluded that there must be an invisible world or there could be no visible world. For something cannot come from nothing.

So the Ancient Astrologers ripped the veil of illusion from the face of the phenomenal world, and found the noumenal world, the realm of reality and permanency.

Their basic teaching was founded on the doctrine, As above, so below.

This earth, while it has shape and substance, and is activated by cosmic force, is only an appearance, an illusion, and may, under certain conditions, be dissipated as a cloud, and transformed into invisible substance, as ice is changed by heat into invisible vapor.

In plainer terms, the phenomenal world is a condensation of invisible substance from a vast, invisible realm that contains everything we see, but existing on a higher octave, beyond the reach of man's five senses.

In the case of man's body, for instance, we are deluded by its appearance. Even doctors don't know that man has four bodies, not one, and these four correspond to the Four Elements symbolized by the Sphinx, fire, air, water and earth, listed by Hotema in "The Breath of Life and the Flame Divine" as astral, aerial, fluidal and physical.

Behold the illusion.

These are some of the secrets of life concealed in the Inner Doctrine of the Ancient Masters, and taught to the Neophyte in the Ancient Mysteries.

This knowledge revealed to man the nature of his own body and soul, and dissipated the obscuring fog which we see with our eyes, and prevents all those who live by sight from realizing what they really see, and are.

It was imperative that the Church destroy the Ageless Wisdom to keep man enslaved in darkness, and make him believe he is a lowly worm, instead of a god, that needs a Savior to salvage his "lost Soul" from eternal torment, as explained by Hotema in "The Soul's Secret".

According to Christianity, the Soul (Ego) is not immortal in its own right, but may acquire immortality if man will entertain a certain belief, — the most preposterous proposition and the basest fraud ever invented.

The Soul that becomes immortal as the result of a certain belief, according to the Mother Church, had no antecedent existence. It was born in the body, and Immortality rises from Mortality if man will believe what the Church teaches.

Those who desire to pursue this line of thought further, should read "The Soul's Secret" by Hotema.

JUSTICE ·   THE HANGED MAN.

Chapter XVII

Card 11, Justice & Card 12, Judgment

Card 11, JUSTICE

The goddess shown in this card indicates the Tarot is not of Greek or Roman mythology. Its presentation of Justice is supposed to be one of the four cardinal virtues included in the sequence of the Greater Arcana.

The woman is seated between two pillars, like the High Priest's, indicating that some aspect of the Creative Principle is involved. This becomes more apparent as we proceed.

The Pillars of Justice and those of the High Priestess open into the same world, but present different aspects thereof.

The woman is a conventional personification of Justice. Her golden hair, like that of the Empress, identifies her with Venus. So does her green cape.

She is also identified with the woman in Card 8, who tames the red lion.

We encounter another trick here. It appears that in the exoteric Tarot, Card 8·is Justice and Card 11 is Strength. This blind does not deceive those who know the attributions of the signs of the Zodiakos to the letters of the Hebrew alphabet.

-143-

Why this trick was ever employed may be difficult to comprehend now. Yet it does serve to emphasize the fact that Cards 8 and 11 present two aspects of the operation of a single principle, which is the Creative Principle symbolized by the High Priestess.

Beneath her purple mantle, showing at the sleeves, is a blue under-garment. This is the color of the High Priestess, and her number is 2, which results from adding the digits of 11, the number of Justice.

In the Rider Tarot, Justice wears a crown, showing three turrets, ornamented with a square jewel. The three turrets and the four sides of the square make the number 7, the Kabalistic number of the Sphere of Venus on the Tree of Life.

The throne of the woman also has, stretched between its two pillars, a violet veil. The Pillars and the Veil are reflections of the ideas suggested by similar symbols in the picture of the High Priestess.

The upright double-edged sword in the woman's right hand is of steel, a metal attributed to Mars. It is an indication that all action is dual, destructive as well as creative.

- - - - - - - - - -

Ouspensky says:

"When I had become possessed of the keys of the High Priestess (Card 2), had read her book, and understood the symbols, I was permitted to lift the veil of the Temple and enter into the inner sanctuary.

"And there I saw a woman seated between the two columns of the Temple, with a golden crown and a purple mantle. In her right hand she held an uplifted sword, and in her left a pair of scales.

"The sight of her made me tremble with fear, because her gaze was deep and piercing.

" 'You are seeing Justice,' said the Voice. 'Everything is weighed in her scales. The sword is eternally lifted in defence of Justice, and nothing can escape it.

" 'Why do you turn your eyes away from the scales and the sword? Are you afraid?'

"Yes, for they deprive you of your last illusion. How will you live on earth without these illusions?

"You wanted to see Justice, and now you have seen her.

"But remember what awaits a mortal when he has seen the goddess. He will never again be able to shut his eyes to that which does not please him, as he has done hitherto. He will see Justice perpetually, always and in everything, and will realize that he reaps as he sows."

- - - - - - - - - -

But the Mother Church teaches that the gospel Jesus paid it all with his blood. That is another falsehood which does its part to fill the world with violence.

The Great Law as Karma grants to each one the portion of goods he merits, and sends him forth into this far country of earthly life, to determine what use he will make of his inheritance.

These goods are all the faculties, powers, knowledge and wisdom gained by the Ego thru past experience, expressed in this earthly life as inherent faculties, powers and abilities, together with the, as yet, undeveloped possibilities which the experiences of this life are intended to unfold.

Only by this unfoldment thru evolution can the Ego be molded and fitted to take its rightful place in the Grand Plan.

That is real Justice.

The Great Law of Justice will keep man in bondage to physical limitation, in the prison house of flesh, in the treadmill of Karma, incarnation after incarnation, until he has fulfilled every jot and tittle of the Law he has broken under the urge of carnal lust.

Simplicius wrote:

"The Pythagoreans said that the same things are repeated again and again. ...Because of movements of the astral bodies and many other things are the same age after age, what occurred before and what will occur afterwards are also the same. This applies also to repetition, which is always the same.

The compilers of the New Testament knew about repetition and made their Jesus speak of it to his disciples.

In the Gospels there are many veiled allusions to this, but the most certain passage, which has quite a definite meaning in the Greek and German texts, has lost its true meaning in translations into other languages, which took that most important word from the Latin translation.

And Jesus said unto them, Verily I say unto you, That ye which have followed me, in the REGENERATION ... (Mat. 19:28).

The word "Regeneration" in the Greek text is "Renovation," according to Wilson's "Emphatic Diaglott."

The basic meaning is Reincarnation, Repeated Existence, Repeated Birth, Born Again (Jn. 3: 3, 5, 7).

And so, the very ancient doctrine of Reincarnation had to be rejected, had to be concealed in "Regeneration," in order to provide a job for the gospel Jesus.

The entire system of Christianity is based on this passage:

"For God so loved the world, that he gave his only begotten Son, that whosoever believeth in him should not perish, but have everlasting life." (Jn. 3:16).

The fact of Reincarnation rips away the foundation of Christianity.

REINCARNATION

If Reincarnation is a fact, a man may be justified in asking: "If such a phenomena as the repetition of lives on earth is true, why do we know nothing of it? Why do we not remember more?

There is a definite reason why the memory of antecedent incarnations so seldom occurs.

In our evolution we have passed thru many sad and embittering experiences which, if remembered in subsequent incarnations, would so depress our Ego - so discourage and hamper us, that we would make little effort to progress.

Also, if we did remember who we had been before, and whom our present companions were, we would find it so hard in many cases to forgive the injuries, so hard to forget the troubles we had gone thru in connection with them, that our progress would be retarded.

Since the Great Law, acting as Karma, demands perfect compensation or adjustment, one great object in each new life is to readjust the mistakes of the past.

Another reason why we do not remember is, at each incarnation the Ego clads itself in a new robe, the brain cells of which have never responded to past conditions, and only when the brain is capable of responding to the memory stored in the Higher Self, can that memory be impressed upon the waking consciousness.

In other words, the personality, per se, cannot remember the past because it has experienced only the present life.

And a further reason is that many of our previous lives have been so unimportant and trivial, that they have registered little of value in the Higher Self, hence have little of importance to remember.

For out of each life, it is only those exceptional experiences and those lessons which have made deep impressions upon us, that are immortalized by being registered in the Real Self.

We must not lose sight of the fact that in our present life we forget many things, remembering only those which, for various reasons, have made the deeper impressions upon us.

Like the memory of our present life, which may be aroused by some particular event, the memory of our past life may be awakened by reading about or seeing the picture of some historical character. This arouses a consciousness of having lived at that time or in that place.

This may give rise to much ridicule, for many in whom the memory of past lives is dawning, seem not to have been lower than rulers, kings and queens or notable characters in history.

There is a reason for this. For, like most mistakes, it is rather a misunderstanding or misapplication of the remembrance than a deliberate attempt to deceive.

In such a case the probability is that the person did live in the period remembered, and perhaps took a prominent part in the events enacted, but he was not necessarily the principle character as he thinks he was when the memory of it returns to him.

In the past he may have been deeply interested in the characters under consideration, and fond of imagining himself in their place. Thus, when the memory is turned to those old times, it awakens the old currents of feeling, and a man thinks he was, in the past, what actually he wished to be.

Card 12, JUDGEMENT

Arcanum 12 presents man suspended by one foot from a gallows, head down, the gallows being constructed of a beam supported on the top of two cut trees, each having six lopped limbs along their length. His hands are tied behind his back, and one leg is crossed behind the other, forming a crude cross, which indicates the four cardinal points of the compass, while the severed branches signify the completion of the cycle of the Sun thru the twelve signs of the Zodiakos, indicating the termination of terrestrial life.

The Labors of Hercules are at an end.

We have found nothing which satisfies us as to the interpretation of this symbolism. The Bible says:

"If a man have committed a sin worthy of death, and he be to be put to death, and thou hang him on a tree, his body shall not remain all night upon the tree, but thou shalt in any wise bury him that day" (Deut. 21: 22, 23).

The biblical makers here inserted this phrase: "For he that is hanged is accursed of God" (Deut. 21:23).

Then they made it appear that this interpolated statement was in the ancient scroll by inserting this statement in the New Testament:

"For it is written Cursed is every one that hangeth on a tree" (Gal. 3: 13).

But it was not so "written" until the biblical makers wrote it, in their crafty scheme of re-shaping the ancient scriptures to serve their nefarious purpose, which was to enslave humanity.

The four fixed signs of the Zodiakos, Leo, Scorpio, Aquarius and Taurus, form the Cosmic Cross on which man hangs in the physical world for evil purposes, using the Sacred Temple in which he should glorify Life, to debase his precious life and to satisfy his lusts for sensation, greed, hate, jealousy, etc.

Because of the position in which man is presented in this card, other commentators call it the Hanged Man. But to us, the term Judgment seems to be a far more fitting title.

Man's experience with himself and mankind in general, as depicted in Cards 6, 7, and 8, being insufficient to teach him the great lesson of Life and constrain him to seek the Light of the Hermit, he appears in Card 11 before the Bar of Justice, is found wanting in the qualities that make a man, and receives the Last Judgment, which is carried out as portrayed in the next card, No. 12.

We have followed the trail of the Man of Darkness from the days of his youth to the time when the harvest is ready, and we see that man reaps as he has sown.

And this is the end of the trail of the gay youth we saw in Card 0, the Fool, who became the Conqueror of cities and nations in Card 7 — but failed to conquer his own animalistic nature.

He now appears before the Bar of Justice where his good deeds as to his own body are weighed against the evil deeds as to his own body, and we behold the result.

The verdict is "Guilty."

Man has failed to fulfill the obligations due to his own body. He has failed to heed the message of the Ancient Masters who said:

Flee fornication. He that committeth fornication, sinneth against his own body. For it is good that a man touch not a woman.

The Bible considers the unition of man and woman in marriage as a condition tolerated and accepted because it is the lesser of two evils. The Bible says:

If they cannot control the generative urge, then "let them marry; for it is better to marry than to burn" (1 Cor. 7: 9).

We shall quote from an essay by Lucinda B. Chandler on Social Purity as to the subject of marriage:

"When a woman has made this agreement (of marriage) ... she has made herself permanently ... a legal prostitute till death or divorce dissolves the contract.

"I demand the immediate and unconditional ABOLITION of this vilest system that ever cursed the earth.

"Marriage is legalized prostitution. ... The term marriage is more offensive that the terms rape, murder, or prostitution, because it involves all of them, and all combined are worse than either alone. ....

"The wife is the most degraded of all prostitutes, ... a forced prostitute ... Popular prostitution, bad as it is, is not so bad as the forced prostitution of marriage." — Sex Worship, Wall, p. 173.

The biblical makers sanctioned marriage and large families. That was necessary to build up a large force of slaves to support and sustain their religious system. So they said this in their Bible:

"Be fruitful, and multiply" (Gen. 1: 28).
-147-

That statement never appeared in the ancient scrolls. It was interpolated by the biblical makers who sought to carry their system to success by guilding up a large membership. To encourage the production of large families, they wrote:

"Marriage is honorable in all, and the (marriage) bed (is) undefiled" (Heb. 13: 4).

But there stands the Edenic Allegory of the Ancient Masters, to the effect that the day man puts himself in the power of the Great Red Dragon (Rev. 12), "thou shalt surely die" (Gen. 2: 17).

This subject is so important that Hotema has covered it in detail in his work titled "Great Red Dragon."

Judgment is not a condition to occur in the future, as taught by the church. The judgment scene is enacted right here on earth, and not in the existence of the Ego after its sojourn here.

Man is constantly in the Scales of Justice here and now, and the execution of the Judgment takes place here and now on the earth.

The Egyptian trial of the Ego and the weighing of the Heart in the Hall of Judgment of Osiris, are scenes located by the old scriptures in Amenta, and the fact should not be overlooked that this Amenta is the Life we live here and now on the earth.

We meet the Book Of Life at birth on the earth, not at death. For we bring with us at birth our past record, written upon our inner ethereal vestures in letters of character.

In this life we face the issues raised by the former good or evil work in our antecedent incarnations.

Christendom owes much of its success to the teaching that man can perpetrate what heinousness he will in this life, and wait a millennium before being brought to the reckoning.

The certitude of the instant judgment, the reaping as we sow, has been obscured or denied by the church.

The Christian is deprived of the definite knowledge and benefit that the consequences of his acts are in the immediate reaction upon him here and now.

The shadow of the law has been deludedly removed from his mind by the church, with the result that life has proceeded largely without any consideration of the certainty of Justice.

And with this sense of immunity bolstered by the concommitant doctrine of a vicarious atonement and the forgiveness of sins, the deluded and misguided mind of the Christian has indulged in such revelries of license and heedlessness as history has never recorded at any other period of the world.

The assurance that the world is ruled by law, that acts carve the shape of destiny, is hardly to be found in the Christian world.

The habitual philosophy of the Christian mind consists of the hazy notion that the theological Day of Judgment, if it is to come at all, is a long way off.

The Christian is not taught that what he gets out of this life comes as the fruit of what he puts into it. He will reap as he has sown.

And this may be bad news also for those half-baked occultists who are looking for "hidden knowledge," for the short cuts and the secret way to the Goal of Seership.

THE GOD FAILS

Upon that strange extravaganza, the curious fantasia, which presents itself as the history and saga of the human species, the judgment of an unprejudiced, uninvolved and remote spectator -- say, an observer of another thinking species or an intelligence of another planet, would be --

Ludicrous, ridiculous failure!

Even the verdict of any sufficiently detached human naturalist, a practical animal breeder or a biologist, taking the measure of his own species, would amount to an extremely low appraisal of its worth and accomplishments.

For, of that top breed of those who are known as the blue ribbons, the firsts, the primates, the aristocrats of the vertebrates, the ultimate birth of time's gestations, placed at the very head of the hierarchy of the living, all that could be averred would be, that Man's utmost endeavors to succeed as a species have attained neither to his expectations nor his aspirations, but were leading only to his degradation, if not his destruction.

The philosophical biologist is the personification of a specific power and tendency of Man, the ability to weigh and measure himself, to subject himself to comparison and appraisal, to laugh and weep at himself and his history as a whole, to look upon himself objectively and critically, and perhaps to learn and change and modify, and even to improve, his own nature.

And because Man possesses self-consciousness, an awareness of his differences and characteristics, he has long asked:

What is Man?

Once having satisfied the cravings and demands of his animal nature, he turns everywhere to a consideration of his humanal nature. From the very beginning of his inquiries into the nature of all things, for his curiosity has always been more than simian, he has returned repeatedly to that final question:

What is Man?

Provisional answers of some sort he has always provided, since he was compelled to integrate them with the practices of his daily rituals, habits and customs by which his elementary needs and drives were satisfied.

Out of his immediate observations and reflections, his dreams and imaginings, he would invent some working theory that served as an answer to his wonderings about himself. Only he never thought of his ideas about himself as provisional theories, but as revelations and intuitions of fixed and absolute truth.

THE GOD'S WRECKED INSTITUTIONS

All any impartial observer need do is to regard the remains of the wrecks of Man's once flourishing nations and empires left behind. They record his pathetic attempts to spread wide and far the domain of protected order and enterprise which he proudly calls his "civilization."

Only one conclusion is afforded: While Man has tried again and again, has strained his energies to build a man-proof civilization, he has failed continuously and repeatedly.

Each one of his civilizations had its bright beginnings and promise of endurance. At its prime it seemed as secure as the earth itself. But because no provision was made, or no steps could be taken, to change for the better the human material which was their substratum, they possessed no lasting vitality.

Man realizes that during the long ages of his adventures, he has contrived a vast multiplicity of the modifications of matter that are his tools and machines, adjuncts to his organs of flesh and bone, his hands and feet, his muscles and senses. And his mind in the substance of his brain has added an almost unmanageable horde of ideas and conceptions to the bare instinct-instruments of his thought.

But not the totality of his achievements has touched the true evils of his life -- only multiplied them. For they have aggregated more and more, so to pain and wound, to hurt and mutilate, to degrade and enslave, to deprive and frustrate, to hinder and retard the amelioration of his fellow creatures, which means himself, so to spoil and ruin the lives of his kind as to make men curse the day they were born.

This, in general, is the substance of part of the story which the Ancient Masters, after a million years of observation and experience, told in the symbology of the 22 Trumps Major, no traces of which can be found either in Egypt or in India.

It was to rescue Man from this darkness that inspired the Masters to found the Ancient Mysteries. And it was to guard the integrity and fidelity of these schools from the superstition of the masses and the usurpation of the priesthood, that constrained the Masters to receive and accept for initiation only those who proved by appropriate tests to be worthy of acceptance.

The esoteric character of the school was preserved by powerful sanctions. An oath of secrecy was administered in the most solemn form to the initiate, and to violate it was considered a sacrilegious crime, the prescribed punishment for which was immediate death.

CONCLUSION

The Mother Church and Medical Art do not want Man to know what he is. For that reason both institutions combine in the scheme to keep him in darkness.

In spite of all the so-called medical research, we shall quote what a great doctor said of medical ignorance as to Man. Dr. Alexis Carrel wrote:

"Man is composed of a procession of phantoms, in the midst of which there strides an unknowable reality . . .

"Our knowledge of the human body is, in truth, most rudimentary. It is impossible, for the present, to grasp its constitution. We must, then, be content with the scientific observation of our organic and mental activities, and without any other guide, march forward into the unknown" (Man The Unknown- pp. 4, 109).

That admitted ignorance on the part of Medical Art is the result of a definite plot to keep Man in darkness as to himself in order to make his enslavement less difficult and more certain.

All efforts by intelligent scientists to clarify the nature of Life and explain the constitution of Man are opposed as vigorously by Medical Art as by the Mother Church. And the reason in both instances is the same.

The work of the Ancient Mysteries had for its purpose the liberation of Man from the realm of darkness by teaching him the nature of Life and the constitution of his body. And that is the reason why they were crushed and destroyed.

According to Iamblichus, a Neo-platonist of the 4th century, the ritual of initiation into the Egyptian Mysteries required the Neophyte to commit to memory, as it was explained to him by the Hierophant, the interpretation of the symbolism of the 22 Arcana of the Tarot.

This interpretation, to be correct, must agree with the ancient philosophy of Life, and that is the interpretation we have presented in this work. In addition, we have included some of the esoteric instruction the Neophyte received. More of it is contained in our other works, in which we have resurrected the Ageless Wisdom of the Ancient Masters.

In referring to the Tarot, P. Christian, in his History of Magic, said the Neophyte was led down a long gallery, supported by caryatides in the form of 24 Sphinxes, 12 on each side.

On the wall between the Sphinxes there were frescoed paintings, similar to those that can be seen in the ruins of the temples of Thebes, capital of Egypt in 2,000 B.C., and especially on an ancient ceiling of one of the halls of the palace of Medinet-Abou, which pictured the 22 Trumps Major.

These 22 pictures faced each other in pairs, and these pairs, according to Ouspensky, were arranged in the order in which we have paired them in this work.

As the Neophyte was conducted by the 22 pictures, he was halted before each pair and given appropriate instruction by the Hierophant as to the esoteric meaning of the symbolism. This meaning we have set forth in our interpretation of the cards.

It was the knowledge of Life and Man revealed by the interpretation of the symbolism of the cards which caused the Church Fathers to destroy them so completely.

THE CHRISTIAN BIBLE

If Christians were familiar with the history of their Bible they would be less willing to put much faith in the so-called "Word of God."

There is no book more reverenced and less known than is the Bible.

The church claims that Christianity is based on the Bible, and that the Bible is the work of "divinely inspired men." The facts of biblical history prove that these claims are false.

The origin of the New Testament is shrouded in much mystery, but that of the Old is shrouded in more.

The writings from which the Old Testament was compiled were gathered by the Egyptian ruler Ptolemy Philadelphus (309-246 B.C.) for his library at Alexandria.

Learned men of all nations and religions resorted to Alexandria, and from them Ptolemy purchased the principal writings relating to their religions.

In that way Ptolemy succeeded in collecting about 280,000 scrolls of ancient scriptures for his library, which was considered the most valuable library in existence.

Unto this day scholars bemoan the destruction of that library, which destruction was necessary to hide the source of Christianity.

In that library, from these scrolls written by unknown men, the Old Testament was first compiled by the committee appointed by the first church fathers.

No one knew who prepared the original scriptures, nor why they were written. They may have been produced as fiction or fable. The church fathers invented the names of the "authors." Then the church claimed these fictitious names represented "inspired men." A bigger lie was never told.

A BIBLE NEEDED

When Constantine founded the Roman State Church in 325 A.D., there was no definite collection of writings called the Bible because there had been no need for any.

The establishment of the church created the need for special literature to support the claims of the church and to mislead the masses. This urgent need for a Bible produced the Bible, and it became the "Word of God."

If Christianity were based on the Bible as the church claims, then the Bible would have been in existence before Christianity was born. History shows that this is not the case.

Had the Bible produced Christianity, the product had been called Buddhism, its true and correct name. In fact, the Christians were first called Kristosites because they were the followers of Krishna, the Hindu Savior.

Christianity produced the Bible, and made the Bible way what it wanted its Bible to say. Among other things, it wanted its Bible to predict the coming of its Christ; and tried hard to make it do so.

There is not a version of what is called the New Testament that is older than the latter half of the 4th century, or the beginning of the 5th century, A.D. If there were older versions, what became of them?

The oldest extant manuscript of the Old Testament is dated 916 A.D. The words contain no vowels, and there were no punctuation marks.

Vowels were first borrowed from the Syrians, and were first inserted in the biblical writings in the 7th century. No one knows whether the right vowels were put in the right places, and no one cared so long as the context supported the claims of the church.

Eusebius of Caesarea (260-340 A.D.), chief speaker and leading supporter of Constantine's scheme to establish the Roman State Church, began to collect literature needed to support the newly created religion and its mythical "Savior."

In this respect he was the actual father of Christianity; and some of his contemporaries said that a bigger liar never lived.

As Eusebius and his helpers compiled the substance of the Bible from the ancient scrolls, they changed, mutilated, distorted, deleted and interpolated to make the writings say what they wanted their Bible to say in order to serve their nefarious ends.

This task was so great that Eusebius died before it was finished, and Jerome (340-420 A.D.) then took up the job.

From the combined efforts of these men and their assistants, there eventually came forth about 405 A.D. the Latin Bible, termed the Vulgate because its language was so common. Vulgar used to mean common people.

POETRY

The scriptures of the Bible were originally poetical, similar to the context of the Egyptian Bible, the "Book of the Dead."

There are still five poetical books in the Bible that were not changed to prose, -- Job, Psalms, Proverbs, Ecclesiastes, and Canticles or Song of Solomon.

These unmetrical hymns, of poetical character,were originally arranged
for chanting, and are still so used in many churches, for the direct purpose
of arousing the emotions and unbalancing the Mind — a trick not difficult to
do when it is known that 90% of the brain cells of the average person are
dormant.

Man's emotions are equivalent to the sum total of his sentient powers.
The scheme of arousing the emotions is to unbalance the Mind and control the
man, causing him to do what he would otherwise not do. Thus, exoteric religion thrives on blind credulity and disordered imagination.

As poetry, the original scriptures possessed an imaginative quality of
thought and a figurative mode of expression. This imaginative and figurative
work, designed to arouse the emotions and unbalance the Mind is now termed by
the church the "Word of God."

It was not until the 15th century that punctuation marks were first used
in the Bible. The semi-colon was not used until after 1582. Then the contents
of the Bible were first divided into chapters and verses, the purpose being to
make easier of execution the fraud of falsification, interpolation, deletion
and distortion.

THE ENGLISH BIBLE

Before the 14th century there was no English Fible. It came into being
under John Wycliff (1320-1384) and his helpers.

They collected material and translated the Vulgate into an English version
in the years 1378-9, deleting, distorting,and interpolating the context to
suit their opinions and purposes.

This work put the Bible within reach of the masses, who were delighted to
learn, for the first time, something about the mysterious "Word of God."

That began the spread of knowledge that caused the power of the church to
show signs of fading. As knowledge spread, the church power weakened.

The more that people learn about the "Word of God," the less faith have
they in the church.

Llewellyn Powys says: In the future Christianity "will dissolve back
into the mist" because "from the beginning (it) has prospered upon lies" (An
Hour On Christianity).

After Wycliff's translation, other versions of the Bible began to appear
so fast, and were changed and distorted so freely, that England, in alarm,
passed in 1408 a law prohibiting translation into English of the "Word of God."

This law was enacted to stop the farce, because the various versions were
so discordant and so contradictory. But it was all the "Word of God."

The law failed to frighten the translators. Distorted editions of the
"Word of God" were prepared secretly until 1517, when Martin Luther shocked
Christendom by nailing his damning theses to the church door.

Luther's expose was so startling that the ban on translations was ignored, and new Bibles flowed freely to the public.

Then came Tyndale. His work on the Bible caused an explosion. He gave the world his English Bible in 1525, prepared after he was driven from England by the church.

It was the most loved and most loathed Bible of them all. The open-minded bought it to read, while the closed-minded bought it to burn; and 6,000 copies of the Bible were burned by the church in a huge bonfire in London.

The church is determined to rule or ruin.

The excitement caused by Tyndale's work inspired Coverdale in England and Olivetan in France to place within the reach of all, versions of the Bible in English, French and German.

At last the misled masses began to learn something of the mysterious "Word of God" which the church had carefully concealed for a thousand years.

In 1568 Calvin gave the world a different Bible, -- but it also was the "Word of God."

Then in 1582 the Catholic version appeared. Other discordant versions appeared in France, Spain, Italy and other countries. No two were alike, but all of them were the "Word of God."

Conditions grew so chaotic that in 1611 the English clergy rose up and decided to stop the farce and clarify the confusing situation.

After more than a thousand years, Christianity and its Bible were still in a confused and mixed up mess.

So 47 English preachers, prejudiced of course, went to work as a committee to make God a Bible. They made it, and they called it the "Authorized King James Version."

It was not "authorized," nor was it a true and correct version from the ancient manuscripts. It was a conglomeration based on the Vulgate, the bishops Bible of 1568, and other writings. But it was the "Word of God."

If the church claim that the Bible is the "Word of God" is what keeps the book in circulation, the interpretation of it differs with the passing of every few generations.

Every author is granted the right to revise his work from time to time. In the case of the Bible, we have no evidence that the alleged author of the book does the revising. The revising is done by the leaders of Christianity, and they make their revisions to promote their religious system.

The revolution of thought that was set in motion in the 16th century by Luther, has destroyed all claims for the fantastic legends that constitute the very essence of Christianity.

THE CHURCH ACTS

The fast fading power of the church caused the Catholic bishops to meet in the Council of Trent in the 16th century to invent ways and means to stem the tide of Protestantism, started by Luther and the Protestant reformers. They voted in favor of the Vulgate as the true "Word of God." The decree stated:

"Now, if any one reading these books in all their parts, as they are usually read in the Latin Vulgate edition, does not hold them sacred and canonical (observe--not 'inspired') and, knowing the aforesaid traditions, does industriously condemn them, let him be anathema" (accursed) (Westcott).

Westcott then adds:

"This fatal decree ... was ratified by 53 prelates, among whom there was not one scholar distinguished for historical learning, not one who was fitted by special study for the examination of a subject in which the truth could alone be determined by the voice of antiquity" (p. 474).

Such are the men who make and build the organized institutions of civilization that rule humanity, both in religion and in politics.

The contents of the various Bibles are not what God said should be there, but what stupid and prejudiced men said should be there. God had nothing to do with it. Man made the Bible, and then called it the "Word of God."

CHRISTIAN WARS BEGIN

The Protestants promptly rejected the Catholic Bible, but accepted the King James Version, which is largely compiled from the Vulgate.

This course so angered the church, that it threatened with eternal damnation all who followed Luther and Protestantism.

Luther struck back, and declared that the Bible, not the church, is the sole source of authority.

The job was done. This position inspired Luther's followers with courage, and the thunder of the Vatican was answered by the thunder of artillery.

Christian armies, for the glory of God and the sake of Jesus, swept over Europe, as they have continuously done since then; and in the roar of cannon, the horrors of battle, the groans of the wounded and the shrieks of the dying, the doctrine of the Prince of Peace, the inspiration of the Bible, and the divine "Word of God" flourished and grew on the blood of the blind supporters of the church and the deceived followers of Christianity.

The world is afflicted with economic, political and religious wars. All are bad, but religious wars are the worst and most useless. They are further evidence to prove that despots use religion, not for the good of humanity, but as a cloak to conceal their real schemes.

Luther's defiance of the authority of the church started the Reformation and the terrible Christian slaughter that followed.

The result of a hundred years of bloody slaughter between Catholics and Protestants on the battle fields of Europe, culminated in the terrible "Thirty Years War" (1618-48), and left Europe desolate and divided on religious lines that remained almost unaltered until 1789, when increasing enlightenment caused Free-thought to succeed Protestantism as the chief rival of the Roman Church.

TOTALITARIAN PAPACY

The Reformation ended the Totalitarian Papacy of the Middle Ages, and brought the enlightenment that was the beginning of the end of the Dark Ages that had settled over Europe when Christianity was born.

Modern Catholicism, unlike medieval Catholicism, has been a defensive organization. The modern Papacy, no longer the unchallenged master of Europe as it was in the Dark Ages, has been reduced to fighting for its existence against the constantly growing modern secular tide of "heresy."

By skillful maneuvering, Roman Catholicism manages to defer its final exit from the stage, and still fights on, haunted by the envisioned glory of its former medieval grandeur.

PREDICTIONS AND PROPHECIES

As we have said, the Bible builders made their Bible say just what they wanted it to say. They predated events to make the prophecies come to pass as predicted. They forged alleged prophecies, particularly those foretelling of their Christ's coming.

An example of these prophecies: "In that day shall there be an altar to the Lord in the midst of the land of Egypt" (Isa. 19: 19).

That altar of stone in the form of the Great Pyramid had been standing "in the midst of the land of Egypt" for thousands of years before that "prophecy" was put in the Bible.

All the alleged predictions and prophecies in the Bible were interpolated years after the events had happened.

That is the fraudulent work that provided Christianity with the "Word of God" which English-speaking nations have circulated far and wide.

During the first fifty years of its existence, the American Bible Society published over 22,500,000 copies of the Bible, or parts of it.

For their English Bible, the Catholics adopted the Vulgate, translated other versions into Greek, and then re-translated the Greek back into English. Then on the title page was placed this misleading inscription:

"Translated out of the original Greek, and with the former translation diligently compared and revised."

Man did this, God had nothing to do with it. He did nothing and said nothing. All Bibles are the same to God. They are the work of man.

There have been more than 1800 conflicting versions of the Bible, compiled from more than 8,000 manuscripts. Which one is the "Word of God?"

BIBLE HISTORY LITTLE KNOWN

The true history of the Bible is little known to orthodox Christians because they refuse to read anything that might "poison" their minds.

If Light and learning will poison our minds, give them to us freely, for we want our minds well poisoned.

This history of the Bible has been dug from ancient ruins left by the church fathers in their efforts to hide the facts about the Bible. It is the work of diligent researchers who were hunting for facts and searching for truth. If the Bible were the "Word of God," they wanted to know it, and not take it for granted.

Christendom has been supplied with its knowledge concerning biblical literature by prejudiced men -- priests, preachers, monks, Christian authors, who frantically support their religious system by selecting and constructing literature most favorable to their cause.

When the writings themselves would not do that, they were altered and distorted so they would do that. The art of printing put a stop to that brand of fraudulent work.

In our histories and encyclopedias we find little but falsehoods about Christianity and its Jesus, written by prejudiced Christians.

Religious articles in the press, the histories, encyclopedias, biblical dictionaries, are rigidly censored by the church to conceal the facts.

The people get but one side of the story, prepared by prejudiced Christians who are under control the same as are the press, the schools, colleges, and the government itself.

THE "WORD OF GOD" BECOMES ESTABLISHED

The Roman Church, in the Council of Trent, decided once and for all what the Bible should contain; and the Westminster Assembly, in 1674, gave the English-speaking Protestants their Bible.

The facts of history show that the "Word of God," as Christendom has it today, is about 300 years old, and that Christianity is the product of evolution. It took from 325 A. D. to 1647 for it to evolve from its embryonic stage to what it became in the 17th century.

It required almost fourteen hundred years for Christianity to collect, revise and edit the literature to make its Bible. It is not the work of divinely inspired men, but of badly prejudiced schemers who have resorted to fraud, forgery, falsehood, corruption, suppression, slaughter and murder for the sake of their religious system.

With these facts in mind, read what the Bishop of Manchester, England, said to his credulous and deceived followers:

"The very foundation of our faith, the very basis of our hopes, the very dearest of our consolations are taken from us, when one line of that sacred volume (Bible), on which we base everything, is shown to be untruthful and untrustworthy" (Bible Myths, p. 17).

There is no limit to what prejudiced Christians will say and do to support their religious system.

NEW TESTAMENT ERRORS

Look Magazine, of February 26, 1952, carried an article by Hartzell Spence titled "The Truth About The Bible," in which he said:

"A study of the New Testament now in progress indicates that much of it, including portions we think of as the very heart of the Bible, were inserted or changed over the centuries, either deliberately or by mistake.

"Students have questioned for centuries the accuracy of many biblical passages. As early as 1720 an English authority estimated that there were at least 20,000 errors in the two editions of the New Testament commonly read by Protestants and Catholics. Modern students say there are probably 50,000 errors."

In that case, then more than one line of the Bible is shown to be untruthful and untrustworthy; and that takes away "from us" the "very dearest of our consolations," as the Bishop of Manchester said.

SKILLFUL WORK

The most remarkable feature of the Bible is the skillful manner in which the compilers wove factism and falsism together.

We defy anyone to read one paragraph in the Bible and find in it either truth or falsehood separately stated.

Each falsehood is inseparably connected with an undeniable truth, and yet the true and the false are so intricately and delicately interwoven, that it is impossible for the unprepared mind to separate the one from the other.

The Bible is the greatest book of distortion, interpolation, fraud, falsehood and misrepresentation that man has ever produced. The purpose of the work was to enthrone the church and enslave the masses.

And so, the Bible has gone out to the world and chained in darkness and ignorance a larger number of people than any other secular book has ever done.

And these deluded victims must live in that error until they shall have evolved to such mental ability that they can winnow truth from falsehood, and come to understand the falseness.

No system of human enslavement which the world has ever known, has been so clever, cunning and complete as that termed Roman Catholicism, and what is called Protestantism is only one short step better off.

-0-

KING of WANDS

QUEEN of WANDS.

KNIGHT of WANDS.

PAGE of WANDS.

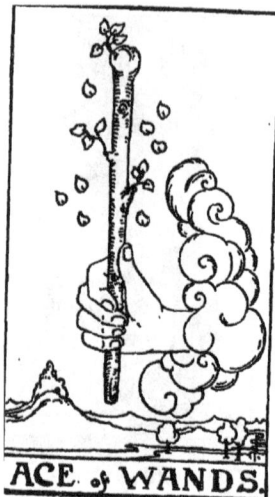

ACE of WANDS.

II

III

IV

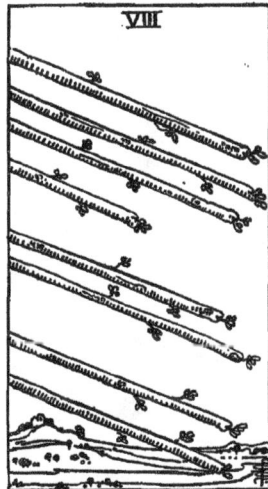

KING of CUPS.

QUEEN of CUPS.

KNIGHT of CUPS.

PAGE of CUPS.

ACE OF CUPS.

II

III

IV

KING of SWORDS.

QUEEN of SWORDS.

KNIGHT of SWORDS.

PAGE of SWORDS.

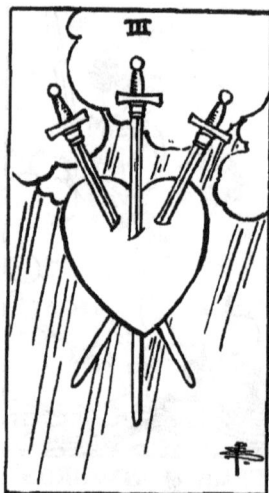

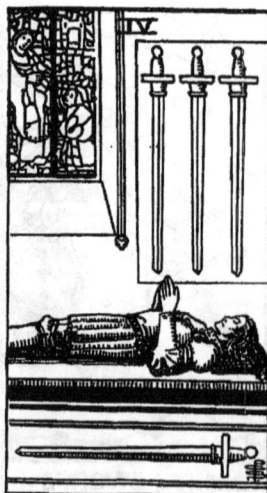

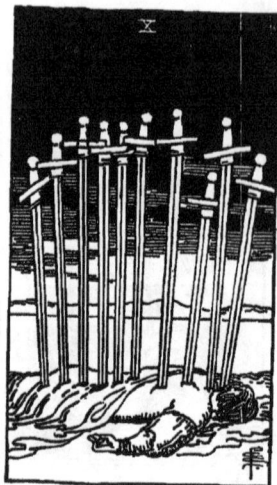

KING of PENTACLES.

QUEEN of PENTACLES

KNIGHT of PENTACLES.

PAGE of PENTACLES.

www.ingramcontent.com/pod-product-compliance
Lightning Source LLC
Chambersburg PA
CBHW050214270326
41914CB00003BA/412